Mexicans

IN MINNESOTA

Dionicio Valdés

Foreword by Bill Holm

MINNESOTA HISTORICAL SOCIETY PRESS

Cover: (front) Faustino and Jorge Avaloz dressed for a Mexican Independence Day celebration on Harriet Island, St. Paul, 1941; (back) Independence Day parade on St. Paul's West Side, 1938

Publication of this book was supported, in part, with funds provided by the June D. Holmquist Publication Endowment Fund of the Minnesota Historical Society.

www.mhspress.org

The Minnesota Historical Society Press is a member of the Association of American University Presses.

Manufactured in Canada

10 9 8 7 6 5 4 3 2 1

International Standard Book Number: 0-87351-520-X

♾ The paper used in this publication meets the minimum requirements of the American National Standard for Information Sciences Permanence for Printed Library Materials, ANSI Z 39.48-1992.

Library of Congress Cataloging-in-Publication Data

Valdés, Dennis Nodín.
    Mexicans in Minnesota / Dionicio Valdés ; foreword by Bill Holm.
        p.   cm. — (The people of Minnesota)
    Includes bibliographical references (p.) and index.
    ISBN 0-87351-520-X (pbk. : alk. paper)
        1. Mexican Americans—Minnesota—History. 2. Migrant agricultural laborers—Minnesota—History. 3. Alien labor, Mexican—Minnesota—History. 4. Minnesota—History. I. Title. II. Series.

F615.M5 V35 2005
977.6'0046872—dc22

                                                                2005041496

This book was designed and set in type by Wendy Holdman, Stanton Publication Services, Minneapolis, Minnesota; it was printed by Friesens, Altona, Manitoba.

Contents

Foreword

by Bill Holm

Human beings have not been clever students at learning any lessons from their three or four thousand odd years of recorded history. We repeat our mistakes from generation to generation with tedious regularity. But we ought to have learned at least one simple truth: that there is no word, no idea that is not a double-edged sword. Take, for example, the adjective *ethnic*. In one direction, it cuts upward, to show us the faces, the lives, the histories of our neighbors and ourselves. It shows us that we are not alone on this planet—that we are all rooted with deep tendrils growing down to our ancestors and the stories of how they came to be not *there,* but *here.* These tendrils are visible in our noses and cheekbones, our middle-aged diseases and discomforts, our food, our religious habits, our celebrations, our manner of grieving, our very names. The fact that here in Minnesota, at any rate, we mostly live together in civil harmony—showing sometimes affectionate curiosity, sometimes puzzled irritation but seldom murderous violence—speaks well for our progress as a community of neighbors, even as members of a civilized human tribe.

But early in this new century in America we have seen the dark blade of the ethnic sword made visible, and it has cut us to the quick. From at least one angle, our national wounds from terrorist attacks are an example of ethnicity gone mad, tribal loyalty whipped to fanatical hysteria, until it turns human beings into monstrous machines of mass murder. Few tribes own a guiltless history in this regard.

The 20th century did not see much progress toward solving the problem of ethnicity. Think of Turk and Armenian, German and Jew, Hutu and Tutsi, Protestant and Catholic, Albanian and Serb, French and Algerian—think of our own lynchings. We all hoped for better from the 21st century but may not get any reprieve at all from the tidal waves of violence and hatred.

As global capitalism breaks down the borders between nation-states, fanatical ethnicity rises to life like a hydra. Cheerful advertisements assure us that we are all a family—wearing the same pants, drinking the same pop, singing and going online together as we spend. When we invoke *family,* we don't seem to remember well the ancient Greek family tragedies. We need to make not a family but a civil community of neighbors, who may neither spend nor look alike but share a desire for truthful history—an alert curiosity about the stories and the lives of our neighbors and a respect both for difference—and for privacy. We must get the metaphors right; we are neither brothers nor sisters here in Minnesota, nor even cousins. We are neighbors, all us *ethnics,* and that fact imposes on us a stricter obligation than blood and, to the degree to which we live up to it, makes us civilized.

As both Minnesotans and Americans, none of us can escape the fact that we *ethnics,* in historic terms, have hardly settled here for the length of a sneeze. Most of us have barely had time to lose the language of our ancestors or to produce protein-stuffed children half a foot taller than ourselves. What does a mere century or a little better amount to in history? Even the oldest settlers—the almost ur-inhabitants, the Dakota and Ojibwa—emigrated here from elsewhere on the continent. The Jeffers Petroglyphs in southwest Minnesota are probably the oldest evidence we have of any human habitation. They are still and will most likely remain only shadowy tellers of any historic truth about us. Who made this language? History is silent. The only clear facts scholars agree on about these mysterious pictures carved in hard red Sioux quartzite is that they were the work of neither of the current native tribes and can be scientifically dated only between the melting of the last glacier and the arrival of the first European settlers in the territory. They seem very old to the eye. It is good for us, I think, that our history begins not with certainty, but with mystery, cause for wonder rather than warfare.

In 1978, before the first edition of this ethnic survey appeared, a researcher came to Minneota to interview local people for information about the Icelanders. Tiny though their numbers, the Icelanders were a real ethnic group with their own language, history, and habits of mind. They settled in the late 19th century in three small clumps around Minneota. At that time, I could still introduce this researcher to a few old ladies born in Iceland and to a dozen children of immigrants who grew up with English as a second language, thus with thick accents. The old still prayed the Lord's Prayer in Icelandic, to them the language of Jesus himself, and a handful of people could still read the ancient poems and sagas in the leather-covered editions brought as treasures from the old country. But two decades have wiped out that primary source. The first generation is gone, only a few alert and alive in the second, and the third speaks only English—real Americans in hardly a century. What driblets of Icelandic blood remain are mixed with a little of this, a little of that. The old thorny names, so difficult to pronounce, have been respelled, then corrected for sound.

Is this the end of ethnicity? The complete meltdown into history evaporated into global marketing anonymity? I say no. On a late October day, a letter arrives from a housewife in Nevis, Minnesota. She's never met me, but she's been to Iceland now and met unknown cousins she found on an Internet genealogy search. The didactic voice in my books reminds her of her father's voice: "He could've said that. Are we *all* literary?" We've never met, she confesses, but she gives me enough of her family tree to convince me that we might be cousins fifteen generations back. She is descended, she says with pride, from the Icelandic law speaker in 1063, Gunnar the Wise. She knows now that she is not alone in history. She has shadowing names, even dates, in her very cells. She says—with more smug pride—that her vinarterta (an Icelandic immigrant prune cake that is often the last surviving ghost of the old country) is better than any she ate in Iceland. She invites me to sample a piece if I ever get to Nevis. Who says there is no profit and joy in ethnicity? That killjoy has obviously never tasted vinarterta!

I think what is happening in this letter, both psychologically and culturally, happens simultaneously in the lives of hundreds of thousands of Minnesotans and countless millions of Americans. Only the details differ, pilaf, jiaozi, fry bread, collards, latkes, or menudo rather than vinarterta, but the process and the object remain the same. We came to this cold flat place so far from the sea in wave after wave of immigration—filling up the steadily fewer empty places in this vast midsection of a continent—but for all of us, whatever the reason for our arrival: poverty, political upheaval, ambition—we check most of our history, and thus our inner life, at the door of the new world. For a while, old habits and even the language carry on, but by the third generation, history is lost. Yet America's history, much less Minnesota's, is so tiny, so new, so uncertain, so much composed of broken connections—and now of vapid media marketing—that we feel a loneliness for a history that stretches back further into the life of the planet. We want more cousins so that, in the best sense, we can be better neighbors. We can acquire interior weight that will keep us rooted in our new homes. That is why we need to read these essays on the ethnic history of Minnesota. We need to meet those neighbors and listen to new stories.

We need also the concrete underpinning of facts that they provide to give real body to our tribal myths if those myths are not to drift off into nostalgic vapor. Svenskarnas Dag and Santa Lucia Day will not tell us much about the old Sweden that disgorged so many of its poor to Minnesota. At the height of the Vietnam War, an old schoolmate of mine steeled his courage to confess to his stern Swedish father that he was thinking both of conscientious objection and, if that didn't work, escape to Canada. He expected patriotic disdain, even contempt. Instead the upright old man wept and cried, "So soon again!" He had left Sweden early in the century to avoid the compulsory military draft but told that history to none of his children. The history of our arrival here does not lose its nobility by being filled with draft-dodging, tubercular lungs, head lice, poverty, failure. It gains humanity. We are all members of a very big club—and not an exclusive one.

I grew up in western Minnesota surrounded by accents: Icelandic, Norwegian, Swedish, Belgian, Dutch, German, Polish, French Canadian, Irish, even a Yankee or two, a French Jewish doctor, and a Japanese chicken sexer in Dr. Kerr's chicken hatchery. As a boy, I thought that a fair-sized family of nations. Some of those tribes have declined almost to extinction, and new immigrants have come to replace them: Mexican, Somali, Hmong, and Balkan. Relations are sometimes awkward as the old ethnicities bump their aging dispositions against the new, forgetting that their own grandparents spoke English strangely, dressed in odd clothes, and ate foods that astonished and sometimes repulsed their neighbors. History does not cease moving at the exact moment we begin to occupy it comfortably.

I've taught many Laotian students in my freshman English classes at Southwest State University in Marshall. I always assign papers on family history. For many children of the fourth generation, the real stories have evaporated, but for the Hmong, they are very much alive—escape followed by gunfire, swimming the Mekong, a childhood in Thai refugee camps. One student brought a piece of his mother's intricate embroidery to class and translated its symbolic storytelling language for his classmates. Those native-born children of farmers will now be haunted for life by the dark water of the Mekong. Ethnic history is alive and surprisingly well in Minnesota.

Meanwhile the passion for connection—thus a craving for a deeper history—has blossomed grandly in my generation and the new one in front of it. A Canadian professional genealogist at work at an immigrant genealogical center at Hofsos in north Iceland assures me, as fact, that genealogy has surpassed, in raw numbers, both stamp and coin collecting as a hobby. What will it next overtake? Baseball cards? Rock and roll 45 rpms? It's a sport with a future, and these essays on ethnic history are part of the evidence of its success.

I've even bought a little house in Hofsos, thirty miles south of the Arctic Circle where in the endless summer light I watch loads of immigrant descendants from Canada and the United States arrive clutching old brown-tone photos, yellowed letters in languages they don't read, the misspelled name of Grandpa's farm. They feed their information into computers and comb through heavy books, hoping to find the history lost when their ancestors simplified their names at Ellis Island or in Quebec. To be ethnic, somehow, is to be human. Neither can we escape it, nor should we want to. You cannot interest yourself in the lives of your neighbors if you don't take sufficient interest in your own.

Minnesotans often jokingly describe their ethnic backgrounds as "mongrel"—a little of this, a little of that, who knows what? But what a gift to be a mongrel! So many ethnicities and so little time in life to track them down! You will have to read many of these essays to find out who was up to what, when. We should also note that every one of us on this planet is a mongrel, thank God. The mongrel is the strongest and longest lived of dogs—and of humans, too. Only the dead are pure—and then, only in memory, never in fact. Mongrels do not kill each other to maintain the pure ideology of the tribe. They just go on mating, acquiring a richer ethnic history with every passing generation. So I commend this series to you. Let me introduce you to your neighbors. May you find pleasure and wisdom in their company.

Mexicans

IN MINNESOTA

A group of children posed with their musical instruments at Neighborhood House, St. Paul, in 1938.

THE HISTORY OF Mexicans in Minnesota has been overwhelmingly a history of working-class people. Mexicans initially came to the state not in search of a better life and permanent homes, but to work, and only a minority of them found a better life and stayed. The vast majority remained for short periods before departing.

During the 20th century, Mexicans were the largest minority and fastest growing ethnic group in Minnesota. The terms "Mexican," "Mexicana," and "Mexicano" refer both to persons of Mexican birth and to those of Mexican origin born in the United States. In Minnesota it is misleading to speak of a Hispanic or Latino population, when according to 2000 census figures Mexicans are 15 times as numerous as the second largest group, Puerto Ricans, and 40 times as numerous as the third group, Ecuadorians.[1] The demographic trends justify the focus of this work exclusively on Mexicans.

Minnesota's first known resident from Mexico was Luís Garzón, who was a musician with the Mexico City Orchestra, which was on tour in the United States in 1886. He became ill while in Minneapolis and stayed behind while the orchestra continued the tour. By 1900 the United States census recorded 24 Mexicans living in Minnesota.

Labor and Migration

The first wave of mass migration from Mexico to the United States took place in the early 20th century, due in part to political turmoil in Mexico. The Mexican immigrant was most often portrayed as a rural peon, an ideal candidate for temporary employment with an expectation of a short stay. Between 1910 and 1940, Mexicans were recruited primarily by three major businesses—railroads, meat-packing plants, and a youthful and still-expanding sugar-beet industry.

The railroads were the earliest mass employer of Mexicans in Minnesota because transportation of goods was of such great importance in the Twin Cities. Yet the number of railroad workers was less than in larger cities like Chicago or those closer to Mexico.

Meat-packing was linked directly to industrialization in the 19th century as techniques for railway transportation, refrigeration, and slaughtering facilities improved. As young men and women left the farms to work in nearby cities and European immigrants joined them, they created a greater demand for meat. In the aftermath of World War I, several thousand Mexicans found employment in packing plants, which became the most important employer of Mexicans in St. Paul.

The sugar-beet industry, however, was the major employer of Mexicans in Minnesota. The production of sugar beets on a massive scale took off in the 1890s, and Minnesota farmers starting growing beets shortly afterward when a factory was transferred from Michigan to Chaska. Soon small numbers of Mexicans were being recruited from Kansas and Nebraska to farms in southern Minnesota. The Minnesota Sugar Company, which changed its name to the American Beet Sugar Company and later American Crystal Sugar Company, quickly dominated sugar-beet production in the state. Through labor recruiters and employment agencies, the company lured fieldworkers from increasingly distant locations, particularly south Texas. It arranged for railroad transportation, offered employment and housing, and set a guaranteed piece rate for field labor. A much greater expansion of sugar-beet production took place when several huge factories were constructed in the Red River Valley, beginning in 1926 at East Grand Forks and later at Crookston and Moorhead and at Drayton, North Dakota. By 1928 more than 7,000 Mexican immigrants were

Young woman working in a beet field near Fisher, October 1937

Towns in Minnesota with Mexican population

working in the valley.[2] It was the first industry in Minnesota in which Mexicans dominated numerically, and popular perceptions quickly became fixed on them as migrant workers.

During the season, workers were housed in worker colonias near sugar-beet factories, including in Chaska, East Grand Forks, and Albert Lea, or in makeshift dwellings and old houses on the farms where they worked. Once the season ended, they commonly returned south for the winter, but increasingly the sugar-beet companies encouraged them to remain near the fields or head to St. Paul or Minneapolis. The companies offered higher rates the following year because they could save the cost of long-distance transportation. Because few jobs were available in the cities, the beet companies often provided advances on the following year's wages to cover rent, food, and coal. As one report noted, the company plan "to keep Mexican beet workers in the territory the year round" offset "the expense and trouble of recruiting a new supply in the Southwest every spring." Mexican families in the Twin Cities would sign new contracts in the spring and be taken by sugar-beet agents to the fields of southern Minnesota and the Red River Valley, creating a cyclical pattern of migration within the state. As a 1939 Neighborhood House report observed: "Theirs is a seasonal occupation in which there are many abuses" and few opportunities for winter work.[3]

In Minneapolis, Mexicans settled primarily in two neighborhoods in the 1920s. According to a 1927 survey, about 125 Mexicans resided in the city, including 35 men, 31 women, and 58 children. Fifteen men worked for the railroads, and most lived near the Milwaukee railroad yards in the Seward neighborhood. There was a second neighborhood around Sixth Avenue North and Fifth Street, just north of the Chicago, St. Paul, Minneapolis and Omaha Railroad tracks. One observer reported that "very few houses are wired for electricity; some have city water hydrants

Spanish mission services were held in this family's home at 802 Lyndale Ave. N., Minneapolis, about 1936.

outdoors and practically all have outdoor privies." Eulalia Reyes, whose parents settled from the sugar-beet fields in the 1920s, recalled, "Here they couldn't find jobs. They were cut off from friends and family."[4] But colonia ties strengthened as families shared work and relaxation and even celebrated a Spanish-language Mass at St. Joseph's Church. In the late 1950s, the neighborhood lost its integrity as a result of urban renewal and the construction of Interstate 94.

A much larger number of Mexicans settled in St. Paul. The West Side, across the Mississippi River from downtown, quickly became the site of the largest barrio in the

This boxcar, shown in 1949, for many years housed a chapel for the Mexicans living in Swede Hollow.

state, while a smaller cluster of Mexicans appeared in the old Swede Hollow neighborhood north of downtown. In a survey conducted in early 1927, St. Paul had 467 Mexican residents, including 187 men, 91 women, and 189 children. Of the men, 38 were railroad workers employed mostly by the Rock Island at Inver Grove Heights and the Burlington yards at Dayton's Bluff, within walking distance of the West Side and Swede Hollow. The Armour, Swift, and Cudahy packinghouses employed 104 adults, 10 others found jobs in miscellaneous work, and 35 were idle beet workers. The West Side was home to a majority of permanent resident Mexicans because only people with little money were willing to live there; the housing stock was poor, residences were interspersed with industrial and commercial units, and the zone was subject to periodic flooding of the Mississippi River. According to a survey by the University of Minnesota it was the largest slum area in the Twin Cities.[5]

United States Department of Labor investigator George Edson conducted an exhaustive investigation of hundreds of Mexican barrios and colonias throughout the United States in 1926 and 1927. He reported that the worst lodging he encountered anywhere in the country was in boxcars provided to railroad workers by the Burlington Railroad in Inver Grove Heights, where families crowded together under horrific conditions.[6]

An institutional life quickly developed in response to the rapid population growth. Perhaps the most important presence was the Neighborhood House, a nonprofit social agency that provided family support, food, health referrals, youth programs, English-language instruction, and child care. Meanwhile, the Catholic church permitted Mexicans to have a chapel, which later became a church, Nuestra Señora de Guadalupe.

The sugar-beet industry took advantage of close-knit Mexican families and was the only major industry in the

Interior of Nuestra Señora de Guadalupe (Our Lady of Guadalupe Church), 186 E. Fairfield Ave., in 1955

region to employ large numbers of children and women. Its own political pressure ensured that labor laws protecting women and particularly children would not apply to agricultural workers. The lack of regulation in the highly regimented, corporation-controlled sugar-beet industry was made possible because politicians, educators, and social workers accepted the notion that Mexicans were migrants who were not attached to local communities and disappeared when the season ended.

The experience of living successively in city and countryside became increasingly common for Minnesota Mexicans during the Great Depression. In 1932, American Crystal loosened paternalistic company welfare policies, no longer guaranteeing wages, providing transportation, or offering credit during the winter. Consequently, county officials faced the prospect of dealing with thousands of unemployed workers and pressured them to leave. A 1936 report from the International Institute of Minnesota stated, "Some communities where they work in the summer refuse to let them remain for the winter."[7] Unable to pay for long-distance travel to Mexico or Texas, they increasingly took the shorter trip to the Twin Cities, where they rarely found jobs but at least could live under the protection of a rapidly growing Mexican community, a familiar language, and more opportunities for children to attend school and obtain health care and social services.

A distinction between Mexicans employed in sugar beets versus urban industries in the early 20th century was clearly evident in family structures. Urban employers overwhelmingly hired young adult males and discouraged women and children generally, while the sugar-beet companies preferred family labor. In the factory districts where Mexicans settled, many years passed before gender balance occurred. Males who remained typically sent for their wives and families or returned to Mexico to find a wife and convince her to come north. Mexican women initially were

A Sunday school class at the Spanish mission in Minneapolis in 1936

fearful and reluctant—they were not seeking opportunities in Minnesota, but rather accompanied their families.

One family history reveals the complexity of the migration process, starting with a man born in 1897 in Tepoztlán, Aguascalientes. In central Mexico he worked for 12 years in the coal mines and two more years in the silver mines before he came to the United States in 1926. At Piedras Negras, Coahuila, adjacent to Eagle Pass, Texas, he was approached by recruiters for the American Beet Sugar Company and worked for a season in the fields before heading to St. Paul, where he spent the winter unemployed. He returned to the beets the following season. In the fall of 1927 he obtained work at Armour for several weeks until he was laid off, but he soon landed another packinghouse job in January 1928 at Cudahy. There he earned 30 cents per hour and averaged about $15.00 per week, while he paid rent in the winter of

$8.00 per month. He was laid off again but promised work when conditions improved and decided not to return to the beet fields.[8] He was one of a small number of recently arrived Mexicans to sever his link with the sugar-beet fields fairly quickly while remaining in Minnesota.

The onset of the Depression hit Mexicans particularly hard. In the cities, most who had jobs were quickly fired, and unemployment levels often exceeded 80%.[9] Many families faced severe hunger and resorted to begging, seeking scraps from restaurants and scouring junkyards for discarded items that might net money to purchase food. Furthermore, because Mexicans primarily were foreigners and migrants and lacked a permanent residence, they had little political influence. As the hard times intensified, they became scapegoats among racist critics, who elaborated on the already entrenched notion that a "Mexican Problem" existed and that they would be better off "returning" to their homeland.

With encouragement from the United States Department of Labor, which was responsible for immigration policies, many local government officials, particularly those responsible for welfare, concocted schemes to rid themselves of Mexicans. They hoped to make employment available to European Americans and to lighten their own skyrocketing welfare costs. As a result of repatriation pressures, the Mexican-origin population of the United States fell by more than one-third and included large numbers of children born in the United States.[10] It was clearly a case of unequal treatment under the law, as no other group was singled out for such handling.

In the fall of 1932, Ramsey County welfare authorities, with assistance from officials from Neighborhood House and the Catholic church, planned a drive to repatriate Mexicans. Their efforts resulted in the removal of at least 15% of the residents of the St. Paul colonia from the country. The scheme was not entirely voluntary, to the dismay of

Neighborhood House officials who were upset that the effort associated them and their clients with hostile welfare agents, who strongly favored repatriation. Employers and government officials later suggested schemes to repatriate Mexicans, including one by the Great Northern Railroad and two by local authorities in 1934 and 1937, the last initiated by the governor of Minnesota. But they bore little fruit, as opposition by many government leaders intensified after the 1932 debacle.[11]

In addition, agricultural employers quickly discovered that unemployed European immigrants and European Americans were unwilling to go to the sugar-beet fields, in part because they earned more on welfare. Welfare officials

---

Separating a Mother and Daughter

Repatriation and increased vigilance at the international border between the United States and Mexico had a profound influence on many families. Federal authorities showed little regard for human rights, even separating parents from their infant children. One case involved a woman born in 1909 in San Pedro Caro, Michoacán, whose mother died during her birth. She spent her early years with her maternal grandparents when her father went to the United States in search of a job. He worked in Topeka, Kansas, for many years until he returned to Mexico with the intent of bringing his nine-year-old daughter back with him, but her grandparents were unwilling to give her up. He then went back to the United States and this time settled in St. Paul, finding employment with the Burlington Railroad in 1920. When she was 15 years old, his daughter demanded to come to St. Paul to live with her father, and she remained with him continuously until 1927, when she made a trip to Mexico for several months to visit her family. By 1928 she was again in St. Paul where she worked at the Cudahy packing plant for 18 months, during which time she gave birth to a child but did not marry. In 1930, on receiving news that her grandmother was dying, she returned to Mexico to bid farewell, leaving her baby daughter behind in St. Paul with her father, who was able to obtain a free rail pass for her to the border. A few months later she headed north to rejoin her father and her baby, a United States citizen by birth, but immigration officials at the border refused her permission to re-enter on the grounds that she was liable to become a public charge. Their claims were not supported by evidence but rather by a popular notion that Mexicans were welfare loafers, although her father had worked for the Burlington for ten years without interruption. He demonstrated that he was a steady worker with no intention of leaving his job and insisted that he could care for both his daughter and granddaughter. He was making $90.00 per month and was one of the few Mexicans in Minnesota who had earned enough to purchase two houses, worth a total of $2,000. Nevertheless, the mother was not permitted entry into the United States.

---

treated Mexicans differently, providing allotments in the winter only on condition that they return to the fields in the spring.[12]

Mexicans in Minnesota in the 1930s increasingly moved to St. Paul as a result of changes in sugar-beet company policies predicated in part on the suddenly vast surplus of available workers and the company's ability to shift social welfare responsibilities to county governments. Although they agreed that a "Mexican Problem" existed, social service providers and teachers did not define the term or how to deal with it.[13] In the case of parents, social workers were most concerned about liability to become a public charge and extremely low levels of naturalization. For children, they focused on adjustment of youth at home, in school, and at work. Some social workers considered Mexicans capable of assimilation, while others did not, but they agreed on the need to keep them in their place and under control. To achieve their ends, they used many devices, including ones from the scientific establishment, which had popularized IQ (intelligence quotient) testing that portrayed

Children paused while eating their lunches at the Guadalupe Day Care Center in 1941.

Mexicans as deficient and health reports that showed them to be transmitters of diseases. The uncritical use of these IQ scores by school administrators and welfare caseworkers had the unfortunate consequence of sharply hindering employment opportunities for Mexicans.

In the 1930s and 1940s, social workers and their clients were much more interested in survival. The International Institute was concerned about a federal ruling that women who were United States citizens would lose citizenship rights if they had married an alien prior to April 22, 1929. The Institute emphasized citizenship as important for many reasons, including eligibility to receive social service benefits:

The García family stood in the beet fields near New Ulm, about 1940.

Practically, since American citizenship has now almost become a form of social insurance, it is important that Mexicans become citizens in order to avoid discrimination in employment, loss of social benefits such as Mother's Aid and Old Age pensions and the threat of deportation which is becoming increasingly a terror to every alien. Even though he is not technically deportable, (and few of them are) the alien *is not sure* that he is *not* deportable, and every day brings fresh evidence of the rising tide of feeling against the foreign-born adding to his insecurity.[14]

The social workers at the International Institute offered a "liberal" challenge to some of the more insidious activities of schoolteachers, administrators, and welfare workers. They commonly demonstrated that poverty was at the root of most of the material problems that Mexicans encountered and that prejudice and discrimination by the dominant population were serious impediments to assimilation. Poverty severely limited school attendance and achievement scores of Mexican youth. The children in one family, an International Institute caseworker wrote to the Board of Public Welfare in 1935, "were unable to return to school this fall because they are in need of clothes and shoes. The parents are anxious to have their children attend school."

Housing and health also concerned social workers, and a 1946 International Institute report concluded, "The housing of the Mexican community remains the worst in St. Paul." International Institute caseworkers found that Mexicans were forced to live in substandard housing and pay higher rents than others. One caseworker complained that, "Tax moneys are being used to pay rent for Mexicans living in hovels condemned years ago as unfit for human habitation and growing steadily worse while the owner is guaranteed his rent."[15] Apprehension about health was often related to fear of the transmission of communicable diseases, including tuberculosis, to the majority population.

International Institute social workers were worried about the negative impact of discrimination against Mexicans in St. Paul. One survey in 1935 reported that "Because of race prejudice, the question of the employment future of the Mexican young people is a serious one." The Institute sought to help find employment. It estimated that at the time, of 344 adult men in St. Paul, 215 had private employment, 70% of whom worked in sugar beets, but it noted, "It is not to be expected that the beet field worker will ever again earn enough in a summer to support his large family through the entire year."[16] Outside of sugar beets, 60 were employed in WPA work relief, 33 in meat-packing (Swift, Cudahy, and Armour); 17 on railroads (mostly on the Burlington), while 13 did miscellaneous work. Among 215 adult Mexican women, reportedly only four worked outside the home, two employed part time in meat-packing, and two with the WPA. The report neglected the large number of women who performed domestic tasks for wages outside the home and the vast majority who worked alongside other family members in the sugar-beet fields.

To assist young Mexicanas, the International Institute adopted a plan: "An idea based on the experience of some committee members that the young women would make good domestic servants—the one occupation not over crowded—and has plans to train a small group of girls for this work as an experiment." The project, referred to as the Mexican Girls Household Training Course, prepared the young women for a job that the social workers considered befitting of Mexican women while allowing them to feel good about finding employment cleaning the homes of the social workers.[17]

In contrast to most other cities of the nation, St. Paul's Mexican population exploded during the 1930s, due to two migration patterns. The first wave involved sugar-beet

A group of women met for classes in English conducted by the Works Progress Administration adult education department in St. Paul in 1936.

workers who were discouraged from remaining on local farms or camps during the winters. A second and even larger wave unfolded in the middle and later years of the decade. New Deal legislation, including the Wagner Act of 1935, stimulated labor organizing, and in several sugar-beet producing sections of the region, both the American Federation of Labor (AFL) and the Congress of Industrial Organizations (CIO) conducted campaigns to unionize workers.[18] Mexicans quickly demonstrated an eagerness to join unions that surprised labor organizers throughout the nation and defied stereotypes of them as union busters incapable of organizing.

In 1937 and 1938, the AFL in St. Paul and the CIO in Minneapolis conducted drives to organize the resident sugar-beet workers of the Twin Cities and quickly signed up most Mexican residents in both cities. To thwart the campaigns, American Crystal turned to a new source of workers, residents of Mexican origin from south and south-central Texas. As Neighborhood House director Constance Currie reported in 1937, "The sugar beet employers have been antagonized by the labor organizers among the resident Mexican groups and were therefore hiring families who had newly arrived from the South." By the early 1940s, several thousand workers were making the annual trek from Texas cities and towns to the fields of southern Minnesota and the Red River Valley by truck. They also began to settle out in nearby small towns and larger cities, particularly St. Paul. Despite the plummeting economy and repatriation schemes, the Mexican population of St. Paul skyrocketed during the Great Depression, to 1,500 by 1936 and 2,500 by 1940. It exceeded 3,000 in 1946, the majority on the West Side.[19]

For Mexicans who came to Minnesota, even among those who stayed, individual decisions were tempered by many factors, including the influence of family members, the instability of employment, and the related difficulty of purchasing land or a home. A participant in the first generation of mass Mexican migration in the early 1920s, Juan Gómez, stated emphatically when he was already nearly 90 years old that he did not choose to come to Minnesota. He had a home and a small piece of land in Mexico, but he stayed because of his family and the need to provide for them, although he found work in the sugar-beet fields very unpleasant. Like many Mexicans who first came, he had little idea what to expect from the labor recruiters, but unlike the vast majority who soon departed, he remained more than 70 years.[20]

As part of the Christmas festivities in 1935, Jesse Cardenas, age eight, took his turn swinging at the piñata.

World War II and Its Aftermath

From the end of the Depression through the late 1960s, the Mexican population of Minnesota changed profoundly. It grew rapidly and became much more diverse, particularly as hundreds of individuals and families came from Texas and Mexico. An increasing number of their children and grandchildren were born and reared in Minnesota. In sharp contrast to the preceding generation, the population achieved gender balance.

At the same time, the work experience changed. In agriculture, the sugar-beet industry lost its centrality, but employment increased overall, especially in several vegetable crops. Within urban industry, many individuals obtained more stable jobs, particularly in factories and meat-packing plants. The improved working conditions and steadier employment stemmed from workers' own collective efforts, highlighted by the unionization drives of the late 1930s. A third employment sector, nonunion shops and factories, provided even more employment but less stable and low-paying work for recent arrivals from both Mexico and Texas. During this era, women continued to find wage-earning jobs primarily in agriculture, while many were lured to large factories during the World War II labor shortage.

During the war years, the dominant culture popularized three images of Mexicans based on work experiences. The first was the "wetback," or undocumented worker, who commonly was portrayed in newspaper editorials as a peon illegally crossing the Rio Grande into the United States. Discussions

Mexicans gathered at Harriet Island in September 1942 to celebrate Independence Day. Among them were the Avaloz family: (back, left to right) Ceasaria, Esther, and Gabriel (wearing a Patriotic Committee ribbon); (front) Faustino, Maria, and Jorge.

Migrant workers tended the sugar-beet fields in the Red River Valley, about 1940.

in the media, among politicians, and even by labor organizers most often considered undocumented Mexicans as a threat to the American way of life and standard of living but rarely focused on the central role of employers in hiring them or on their positive contributions to the nation's economy. The discussions and debates, in which Mexicans rarely if ever participated, generally neglected remedies involving human rights, the possibility of granting residency to Mexican immigrants, or ensuring them the same rights of other workers.

A second popular image focused directly on agriculture and could be attributed to the expansion of the "migrant stream" during and after the Depression. It portrayed migrant workers as individuals who followed the crops and quietly departed when the harvest ended, making no impact on the communities where they worked and lived for much of the year. The term migrant worker was used to identify both foreign-born individuals and United States citizens of Mexican origin. The image reinforced assumptions that Mexicans were not rooted in the region, were neither residents nor citizens, did not contribute to the economy or society, and consequently were not entitled to the rights and privileges of "American" workers. For the rest of the century, particularly in rural locations, the media used the terms "migrant" and "Mexican" almost interchangeably.

A third media image was of the "invisible" Mexican, whether individuals were also portrayed as "wetbacks," migrants, or industrial workers employed in unionized settings. This image was particularly important in distracting public attention from the settlement process and the successes of those Mexicans who worked in factories. They were the beneficiaries of two sets of circumstances—the Depression and the drive to unionize workers in industry. These Mexicans simply were "not seen" by others.

The war had a profound impact on Minnesota Mexicans. Paralleling trends elsewhere in the nation, Mexican men participated in the armed forces at extremely high rates. Oral histories, social work records, and other documents record numerous instances in which brothers entered the military, and all of their sisters were married to men in the service.[21]

Several factors might explain such high rates. While some observers have emphasized cultural factors, including machismo, those who point to political, economic, and demographic factors make more compelling arguments. As a young population, Mexicans were susceptible to the draft. Lacking deep roots, political influence, or a middle class, they were seldom eligible for deferments based on employment, as members of farm families, or connections on draft boards. Another possible explanation is a high degree of loyalty toward the United States. Agents of Americanization—school officials, settlement house staff, and welfare caseworkers—would have considered themselves successful by inducing strongly pro-United States attitudes among young men and convincing them to enlist.

The entry of men into the armed services helped bring Mexican women into the wage-labor force—whether or not they were eager to enter. As many others have documented, women handled their jobs admirably, working in ammunition and airplane factories, packing plants, and other industries that earlier had been deemed men's work, only to be pushed out after the war ended.[22] But most were still relegated to tasks long designated as Mexican women's work—either in household tasks or alongside their families in the fields.

A major consequence of so many young men entering the armed forces was an acute labor shortage. Employers again started luring workers from Mexico to fill jobs in agriculture, in factories, and on the railroads. They faced opposition from labor unions and a Mexican government critical of the mistreatment of its citizens during the 1920s and Depression and fearful that, without protection, conditions would worsen for all workers. In order to quiet critics and protect the workers, the United States and Mexico signed a formal agreement in 1942 creating the Bracero Program that would bring Mexican workers to the United States temporarily under the protection of contracts enforced jointly by the governments of both countries. A small number of industrialists, several railroad companies, and agricultural employers, most importantly the cotton and sugar-beet industries, took advantage of the program, whose agricultural component continued through 1964.

Minnesota employers participated in the Bracero Program between 1943 and 1947, when several thousand Mexicans worked under contract on the Great Northern and Northern Pacific Railroads, in fields producing for the

Mexican migrant
workers harvested
asparagus near
Owatonna in 1955.

American Crystal Sugar Company, and in canneries and
fields controlled by Minnesota Valley, Green Giant, Fairmont, and Owatonna Canning companies, and the Hollandale Farm Labor Association, working in vegetable packing
and detasseling seed corn.[23]

After the war, agricultural employers turned increasingly to migrant workers from Texas, rather than ones
from Mexico, to work in the sugar-beet fields in the Red
River Valley and the canning industry of southern and
southwestern Minnesota. In contrast to the sugar-beet
industry, the canning companies, composed of both independent enterprises and major corporations, had less-
centralized operations. Production and the work process
in the fields and the canneries were much more variable
than in sugar beets. Employers based their recruitment on

specific local needs and the degree to which they were able to find local youth and women for seasonal employment. The companies often operated through agencies or company recruiters who promised workers employment, housing, and a guaranteed piece rate for tasks in the fields.[24] Increasingly employers were able to use other means of recruitment, including local advertising, labor contractors, or a word-of-mouth network.

After the asparagus was picked, workers packed it in crates.

Concern over poor treatment of workers, and particularly the lack of systematic care for young children left to fend for themselves in worker camps or in the fields, encouraged the National Council of Churches' Migrant Ministry to establish centers in several locations, including Crookston, Fisher, Moorhead, Ortonville, East Grand Forks, Fairmont, Hollandale, Glencoe, Hector, Buffalo Lake, and Owatonna. Local volunteers and a handful of paid employees provided

A group of children of migrant farm workers played outside at a camp in Minnesota in 1960.

for social and educational needs that state and local government bodies had neglected and that reduced costs to employers.[25]

The vast expansion of migrant labor after World War II was consistent with one important reality in the state. The relatively tiny proportion of settlement by Mexicans in small towns distinguished Minnesota from rural locations in the Southwest, the West, and many parts of the Midwest. It helped reinforce a pervasive institutional rural racism among European Americans and European immigrants who owned the fields where the migrant workers were employed. As of 1946, the Mexican-origin population of Minnesota outside of the Twin Cities was estimated at only 600.[26]

St. Paul continued as the center of Mexican life in Minnesota. The packinghouses became a focal point of reference for a large portion of the barrio's residents. A 1946 study reported that 25 women were employed outside the home, with 14 of them in packinghouses, five in textile mills, and six in miscellaneous employment. Among men with gainful work, 110 were employed in packinghouses, 66 in sugar beets, 30 in railroads, 20 in textile mills, and 44 in miscellaneous employment.[27] It marked a sharp contrast with 1936, when only 35 of 1,500 people were employed in the packinghouses and most barrio residents were sustained by seasonal employment in the sugar beets.

In the aftermath of World War II, more Minnesota Mexicans found steady employment than ever before, although a larger percentage still were relegated to unsteady and seasonal work characteristic of the earlier generation. When they obtained jobs in factories, men still had practically no mobility into skilled industrial employment, the trades, the professions, or even service industries. Mexican women did not become schoolteachers, typists, or secretaries and rarely could find employment as salesclerks or waitresses. Even young women with work experience in Texas were barred from such employment.[28] Midwestern Mexican women were discouraged from enrolling in training courses, and the few who did enroll and graduate from study programs found it almost impossible to find employment in those job sectors. Consequently, there were sharp limits to Mexican

Packinghouse Workers

Many young men got jobs in the packinghouses after completing stints in the armed services. Some observers assert that the men took the jobs because they preferred the easy option of quick money to an apprenticeship in the trades. Yet Mexican men commonly were discouraged by employers and were not supported by union leaders when they sought entry into the skilled trades. A revealing case involves a man born in Mexico in 1907 who entered the United States through Laredo with his parents in 1918, obtained a job there in a greenhouse for two years, then went to Waco where he worked a year as a bus boy in a café. In 1920 the family moved to St. Paul, and although he was only 13, he worked for a few months as a laborer and then at the Armour packinghouse in the hide collar department. A few months later he gained employment at Swift in the bone house, but "The boss was so mean he quit his work." In 1923 and 1924 he was a bus boy in two cafés simultaneously and in 1925 returned to the packinghouse at the Cudahy plant in Newport where he worked in casing for more than ten years. In 1940 he sought to become a tailor and took an eight-month course in busheling and pressing. Although he was rated an above-average student and his instructor asserted that he would fare well as an assistant in a tailor's shop, not a single tailor in the Twin Cities was willing to hire him. Like most Mexican workers of his generation, he stayed on the job not because of the desire for "big money" but because of the "glass ceiling" in employment. In St. Paul, packinghouses were the best jobs they were allowed, with the compensation of friendship and camaraderie of other Mexicans in the work place.

Families gathered for celebrations, particularly weddings. Kenneth and Alice García and several attendants posed for a formal portrait on the West Side in St. Paul, about 1939.

dreams of upward occupational mobility, which had a critical influence on their institutional Americanization.

As a result of greater security of employment and stability of residence, Mexican children were attending school more often, but their achievement record was still dismal compared with the majority population. The first student from the barrio to attend college began her studies in 1941 and dropped out the following year although she had performed well. Young people who had little encouragement to continue their education might become a problem, but police marveled at the low levels of crime and delinquency among Mexican youth, given their poverty and the reputation that the West Side had gained as the worst neighborhood in the Twin Cities.[29] The near absence of social deviancy was the result of close-knit families, tight community bonds, and conscious parental acceptance of responsibility for the public behavior of their children.

NUESTRA SEÑORA DE GUADALUPE
CAMPO DE JUEGOS

A group of boys played baseball at the playground at Our Lady of Guadalupe Church, about 1950.

The Chicano Movement and Farm Workers

The 1960s and 1970s were marked by a rise in social and ethnic consciousness throughout the nation. Among Mexicans
this took form as the Chicano Movement. Contrary to assumptions by many scholars, the movement in Minnesota
was not imported from California, New Mexico, or Texas.
Although influenced by events elsewhere, it began locally,
largely in response to the destruction of the barrio on the
West Side in 1960 and 1961. The West Side had always been
subject to spring flooding. In spring 1952 record-setting
floods inundated the flats, and officials decided the time had
come to confront the flooding problem and clear the area.
The decision stimulated neighborhood residents to act, resulting in protests, demonstrations, and collective calls for
action.[30] Their efforts helped make possible the creation of
a new and even more vigorous Mexican neighborhood and

Two men stood thigh-deep in floodwater in front of the Kenneth García house at 320 Tennessee, St. Paul. In April 1952, the Mississippi River overflowed its banks and inundated the West Side.

business district just uphill, along Concord Terrace. This response soon merged into the Chicano Movement. Many neighborhood activists later became involved in broader national struggles like the United Farm Workers grape boycott and local disputes including the formation of the Chicano Studies Department at the University of Minnesota.

In 1969 there were known to be only four Mexican-origin students among the 50,000 enrolled at the sprawling Twin Cities campus. After calling attention to the lack of a Mexican presence on campus, the students realized that university administrators were unwilling to comply with its stated mission of providing for the concerns and needs of all Minnesotans. Lacking a presence or political power, they initiated a campaign against the university, where Mexicans, African Americans, and Native Americans were vastly underrepresented.

The students demanded that the university launch programs of recruitment, retention, cultural activities, and classroom education, the latter in the form of establishing a Chicano Studies Department. After three frustrating years of meetings, reports, public protests, and demonstrations, university administrators finally acceded. Community and student interest in the department increased, and by 1978 it had six full-time faculty members. But as a broad political reaction set in, university administrators, under the guise of funding shortages, commenced an internal discussion over the appropriate function of education. Hidden in the rhetoric were decisions aimed at the reduction of programs or elimination of outspoken individuals engaged in critical teaching and scholarship.[31]

There had long been an internal debate at the top levels of the university over whether its mission required that there be minority faculty and students to make free expression possible on campus, and those who answered in the negative continued to gain sway through the 1980s and 1990s, often covering their failures by pointing to a commitment to "diversity," an amorphous term that could be manipulated as needed. Yet in 1999, members of the board of regents discussed data revealing that the university ranked 10th or 11th in the Big Ten in terms of Chicano/Latino student enrollment at the graduate and undergraduate levels and among faculty. The data were even more telling given that the University of Minnesota was located in an urban setting, where Chicanas/Chicanos concentrated. While the Twin Cities population reached an estimated 12%, Chicana/o and Latina/o student enrollment and faculty numbers were less than 2%.[32] The university failed to add a single new member to the department faculty for 20 years and allowed attrition, retirement, and broken promises to wear down and frustrate remaining faculty. By 2004, it was slowly rebuilding a once-flourishing program.

A brighter page in the lesson book came from students at St. Cloud State University, where many years of discussion and efforts to attract Chicana/o and Latina/o faculty and create a Chicano Studies curriculum finally bore fruit. Led by members of the Movimiento Estudiantil Chicano de Aztlán (MEChA), students staged a hunger strike beginning on the Cinco de Mayo, 1995. They also contacted politicians, organized community support, staged rallies, and performed on the steps of the state capitol in St. Paul. Their public efforts attracted attention throughout the state and the nation and forced the university to create a Chicano Studies Program and hire several full-time Chicano and Latino professors to develop and offer a coherent program of study and establish a cultural presence at the university.[33]

Accompanying the unfolding of the Chicano Movement was a flowering of cultural activities. A major setting for its expression was the Twin Cities, where writers, poets, visual artists, musicians, and theatrical and dance groups congregated. Some of their efforts were short-lived, while others survived for several decades. They presented visible, public expressions through street art, massive murals, educational efforts, and community theater, produced within and on behalf of the Mexican community.

The notable cases of success included the formation of Teatro Latino de Minnesota in 1981, inspired by the California-based Teatro de la Esperanza. Founded by workers, students, artists, and teachers, it has produced and performed a dazzling array of original works about Minnesota. A dozen years later the Teatro del Pueblo appeared, also offering a rich and varied fare. Other independent artists established CreArte in 1999, aimed at encouraging artistic expression and offering a venue for artists to display their work and provide education at various levels. In recent years artists have drawn attention to the Diá de los

One group that organized in the 1960s as part of the growing cultural awareness was the Brown Berets, who formed to help people and fight racism. In 1972 a chapter marched in the Independence Day parade in St. Paul. At the front of the contingent were young men carrying a statue of Our Lady of Guadalupe, the flags of the United States and Mexico, and the La Causa flag, which was the banner of the Brown Berets.

Muertos (Day of the Dead) on November 2 and a greater awareness of Mexico's indigenous roots and cultures.[34]

The Chicano Movement in Minnesota was closely linked to farm-worker activities on both the national and local levels. In early 1966 the National Farm Workers Association, predecessor to the United Farm Workers of America (UFW), set up its first boycott activities in the Twin Cities aimed at convincing consumers not to purchase and stores not to sell grapes unless they were picked under union contract. Chicano/a students and other Twin Cities residents supported the union's educational and boycott activities. But neither the UFW, with allies in the labor movement, nor independent groups of local farm workers tried to form a union for agricultural workers in the state. Consequently, the farm-worker movement in Minnesota was less confrontational than in many other parts of the nation. The primary struggle involved the law and legislation, as growers focused their attention on the changes sought by agencies and organizations, acting on behalf of migrant farm workers.

Advocacy organizations concentrated primarily on educational programs aimed at providing alternative employment for settling-out farm workers. Migrants in Action and Migrants, Incorporated, focused on education and the settling-out process, overlapping in functions with the Minnesota Migrant Council, which later became Midwest Farmworker Employment and Training. Local organizations sought local and federal funds that had become available through the War on Poverty programs and often established relations with schools and technical colleges. The objective was to encourage settled-out workers to take courses to improve their opportunities for long-term employment.[35]

Despite their modest goals, the organizations frequently drew the wrath of growers and residents of many small towns. Growers even stymied programs that could not be considered controversial, including classroom education. While the growers claimed they did not oppose the classes, "they disliked having young women recruited from their labor crews to serve as classroom aides." As newspaper reporter Bob Goligoski observed in 1969, local farmers "suspected that the lessons might be an effort to organize the workers into some kind of union," and the pressure forced teaching staff and administrators to "act very cautious . . . for fear of alienating the farmers once again." Grower Ray Redmer of East Grand Forks told a reporter in 1971: "If you have anything to do with organizing our Mexicans you can leave right now. They're happy and we're happy, just as things are."[36]

Nevertheless some farm workers and a few advocates were not willing to allow growers to speak and act on their behalf. They found an increasingly sympathetic reception in the press. Rather than presenting stories about farm workers based exclusively on employers' portrayals of satisfied and happy workers, some investigations revealed the ineffectiveness of protective legislation, even pointing out glaring abuses by growers and camp operators. Voices of Chicana and Chicano workers appeared more frequently, expressing dissatisfaction and sharpening class tensions in rural communities. In a 1978 article, reporter Randy Furst described terrible conditions in one camp and included segments of an interview with worker Roberto Guerrero, who urged him to "talk to the people. . . . When I asked for more money, they told me to go away and never come back. . . . Every time I have demanded a just wage they call me a troublemaker. . . . There are some ranchers that treat their workers pretty good. That's about 25 percent of them." Another farm worker, Gilberto Herrera, reminded Furst that politicians would never pass effective legislation because "they have to fight for the rich people because the rich people put them there."[37]

The most important and contentious issue in the state for many years continued to involve migrant worker housing. The state of Minnesota had first passed a law regulating migrant housing in 1949, but it was never enforced and did not lead to a single fine for failure to comply with the weak standards it set. As one migrant worker recalled of his experiences in the late 1950s and early 1960s, "the living quarters in the migrant camps fall generally below slum levels," with a "general atmosphere of filth and neglect." Farmers and their organizations lobbied vigorously to prevent the enactment of amendments to strengthen the legislation. In a tour by members of the Minnesota Industrial Commission in 1955, limited in its effectiveness because a labor recruiter for American Crystal Sugar Company accompanied them, the

The Minnesota Governor's Human Rights Commission documented conditions in migrant camps in 1957 and 1958. The government worker commented on the lack of screens in the windows but said nothing else about this one-room house.

inspectors nevertheless found that at least 75% of migrant labor camps they visited failed to meet standards established in the Minnesota labor code. In later discussions, they declined to conduct additional inspections because they were "concerned about jeopardizing by such inspections the good relations that had been established with employers and migrants after years of work."[38]

Pressure from farm-worker advocates intensified, and in 1969 the Minnesota State Board of Health adopted new regulations on migrant housing.[39] But growers complained that new provisions, including a requirement that hot and cold running water be provided within 400 feet of each dwelling unit, were unreasonable and unfair. Their political pressure ensured that the new legislation would remain as ineffective as its predecessor by preventing the inclusion of a compliance mechanism or requiring inspections.

Farm-worker advocates did not give up, and with the assistance of several sympathetic investigative newspaper reports that exposed horrible conditions in migrant camps, new amendments included a provision for camp inspections. But as another investigation by the *Minneapolis Star* demonstrated in 1978, the problem was not merely a lack of housing inspectors. The reporters discovered more violations in only three camps in Polk County than state inspectors found in visits to 119 camps in the same county.[40] They also found that federal investigators had even warned

Two children showed how to work the pump that served several workers' houses as the sole source of water in 1957.

Migrant workers at the Green Giant cannery near Le Sueur lived in this camp in 1950–55.

camp operators in advance when field inspections would take place, allowing them to prepare for temporary compliance. It was abundantly clear that agents of the state charged with camp inspections still were beholden to agricultural interests and routinely disregarded widespread violations of the law by camp operators.

Employers also joined in a broader nationwide strategy headed by the American Farm Bureau Federation and its affiliates to use the threat of mechanization in order to eliminate workers if more stringent regulations were enacted and enforced. The debate over agricultural mechanization peaked in Minnesota in the 1960s and 1970s as representatives of agricultural interests predicted that mechanization would proceed rapidly with the enactment of additional laws. The president of the Southern Minnesota Beet Growers Association, Virgil Mellies, told a newspaper reporter, in response to a legislative defeat in 1969, "It is going to be almost impossible for us to conform to the new regulations. . . . I think these new regulations are going to take us right out of migrant labor and put us right into the thinning machines." The reporter challenged grower assertions, observing that "Many of the growers used their prognostications as a rationale for not improving their migrant labor camps, hundreds of which were, and still are, being operated in violation of state health department regulations."[41] While mechanization reduced the demand for workers nationwide, in Minnesota, despite the laws, the demand for migrant workers rose sharply because of an intensification of sugar-beet growing in the Red River Valley, which had become the leading producer in the nation.

Farm-worker advocates' efforts to strengthen enforcement provisions received a boost when a group composed of officials from the Minnesota Department of Health and members of the state senate and house made a tour of migrant camps in August 1973. Members "decried the overcrowded, often squalid camps." The prodding forced another series of camp visitations in October 1974 by six members of the Minnesota Board of Health, who "chastised state health department officials for approving the poor quality of the housing." Board of Health member Bridget Coleman was highly critical, asserting that "Only one of the many farms we visited had migrant quarters fit for human habitation. The growers have better housing for their machinery and better barns for their animals." During the visit board members were insulted and treated disrespectfully as one farmer peppered them with abusive language while another ordered them off his property. Nevertheless, board members realized that migrants were reluctant to complain, not because they were happy with conditions, as farmers had asserted, but as another Board of Health member realized, "because they fear they will lose out on work next year." In 1974 the Minnesota Board of Health for the first time in its history actually ordered a migrant camp shut.[42]

Stricter regulations soon appeared at the federal level, and in 1976 the Occupational Safety and Health Administration (OSHA) set standards for migrant housing. Employers who provided housing had to ensure that it was clean, with water and toilets approved by local health departments, adequate lighting, showers, and first-aid supplies. It had to be separated from animals and have sufficient space to prevent overcrowding.[43]

Growers intensified their complaints that the housing standards were too costly to maintain, and they openly resisted the new regulations. Melvin Nagel of Arlington Growers was jailed in 1978 for one month after repeated violations of wage and housing regulations over a period of 15 years, an event that made headlines because it was the first time a grower was jailed for violating any statute protecting farm workers.[44]

Although many camps still were not inspected regularly, irate growers were incensed by their perceived loss of control. When American Crystal changed ownership from a New Jersey firm to the Red River Valley Sugarbeet Growers Association, a cooperative, in the early 1980s, it ceased direct recruitment and contracting of workers and no longer provided for housing, requiring farm workers to fend for themselves. By eliminating housing, growers thus avoided liability. As Southern Minnesota Legal Services attorney Bob Lyman observed, "More growers are knocking down their housing so they don't have to fix it up. More migrants are being forced into town." A temporary housing shortage ensued, and many workers who were unable to find lodging in nearby hotels, apartments, or old houses had to sleep in their vans and pickups.[45]

The tendency was also hastened by several factors related to production. In many cases, crops were shifted to new locations, including asparagus fields near Brooten, pepper fields near Olivia, and cucumber fields around Marshall, Cosmos, Courtland, and Nicollet. In other locations, hand operations intensified as a result of a shift back from mechanical and chemical inputs, in particular leading to an increase of hand weeding of soybean fields throughout southern Minnesota. According to one report, "Farmers say the cost per acre for herbicides in the sugar-beet fields is about the same for migrants. . . . Not all migrants are perfect workers, but herbicides need rain at the right time to work. Otherwise the investment in weed control is wasted."[46]

Growers in the areas where production was expanding and growers who had little prior experience with migrant workers were often less willing to provide new housing, compelling workers to fend for themselves. The change was abrupt, as sugar-beet growers in the late 1970s still included single-family dwellings on their isolated farms as a condition of employment. By 1992, according to a survey by the Red River Valley Sugarbeet Growers Association, 61% of growers had ceased to provide housing.[47]

The increased role of government and nongovernment organizations, along with the impact of the Chicano Movement, led to the appearance of different types of organizations and agencies that dealt with Mexicans in Minnesota. Unlike the earlier ones that were typically under the control of the Catholic Church or social service providers, the new agencies were commonly organized by and on behalf of Chicanos who were rooted in the movement. The volunteers formed Chicanos Venceráin in the late 1960s. They organized social and cultural activities while addressing issues that included education, employment, and police brutality. Members found it difficult to meet the many concerns of the community, and under the

In 1974, about 7,000 migrant workers came north to the beet fields in the Red River Valley. Late spring rains delayed the planting so for several weeks there was no work for them. By the end of June, these workers could begin hoeing the young plants.

leadership of Professor Marcela Lucero Trujillo of the Chicano Studies Department at the University of Minnesota, they gained foundation support from the Urban Coalition to create the organization that became the Centro Cultural Chicano in 1972, renamed Centro in 1999, the oldest surviving Latino social-service agency in the state. A parallel social-service agency formed in St. Paul, Chicanos Latinos Unidos en Servicio (CLUES), that later expanded to offer services in Minneapolis.[48]

Many other agencies addressed specific needs, including health and legal services. The West Side Community Health Services, popularly known as La Clinica, offered health services to the working-class community, with a particular mission of providing services to uninsured and Spanish-speaking clients. Many years later the Centro de Salud also opened in South Minneapolis. These health agencies kept costs down by using nurses and volunteer doctors as much as possible while relying on grants from foundations and the government for support. The need for health care was particularly pressing, as hospitals and clinics typically lacked Spanish-speaking staff and were reluctant to admit patients without insurance. One study completed in 2000 found that the uninsured rate for Latinos in the state was 27%, compared with only 5% for all residents of the state. In 1981, Centro Legal, a nonprofit legal office, was formed to provide for the legal needs of the poor of the Twin Cities' Latino communities, particularly on issues pertaining to immigration, employment, family law, domestic and children's law, naturalization, government benefits, and housing. The creation and growth of nonprofit agencies met just a fraction of community needs, the research group HACER reported in 2001, noting that there were only about 40% as many nonprofit agencies serving primarily Latino constituents compared with the smaller Asian American population of the state.[49]

Nuevos Horizontes / New Horizons

A new cycle in the history of Mexicans in Minnesota was ushered in by profound economic, political, and cultural shifts in the nation and the world in the 1970s. Popular observers, reports, and academics forecast economic decline and limited opportunities, suggesting few inducements for ongoing migration of Mexicans, who seemed destined to become a declining population in a moribund region. In sharp contrast to the forecasters' expectations, the Mexican population of Minnesota soared. Its growth was markedly different from that of the European American and African American populations and was the most significant and unexpected demographic feature in the state.

Several popular explanations have been offered to account for this growth. They include demographic-inspired interpretations emphasizing national trends; push-pull accounts; arguments based on Minnesota's liberal welfare policies; network theories suggesting the central role of recent settlers in luring relatives and friends; and interpretations linked to changes in the national and global economy.

A popular demographic interpretation suggests that the expansion of the Mexican population of Minnesota simply reflects the growth of the Mexican population throughout the nation. With more Mexicans available, employers began to hire them to fill the state's chronic shortage of unskilled labor.[50] Unfortunately the interpretation is imprecise and pays little attention to specific geographic areas. Within the region, Mexican migration was the most important factor in accounting for the demographic increase. In Minnesota, Mexican population growth was not particularly impressive in the 1970s but accelerated afterward, and during the 1990s it nearly trebled, a rate substantially higher than the national average.

Push-pull accounts have posited that the push of economic problems in Mexico and the Texas-Mexico border region beginning in the mid-1980s combined with the pull of jobs in Minnesota, with the added attraction of Minnesota's high quality social services and school systems. Employers and journalists in almost every Minnesota community similarly interpreted the influx as a result of a push from South Texas and Mexico and a pull by the north, "particularly in southern Minnesota, [which] has opened up year-round jobs in the region, even created pockets of worker shortages."[51] Push-pull interpretations have a number of serious flaws, particularly their haziness about why workers would come from South Texas or Mexico rather than any other low-wage region or they would settle in Minnesota rather than somewhere else.

Another popular interpretation of the rapid growth of Minnesota's Mexican population focused on the state's liberal welfare policies. Dodge County Auditor Steve Gransee

Jesus Mendes holding Jesus, Jr., at the Chris Brothers camp near Hollandale, 1958

asserted that Mexicans were willing to work for minimum-wage jobs because they could augment their earnings through the county welfare system. In 1989 a letter to the editor printed in the *Fargo Forum* stated that for migrants to the area, "The first stop once they reach Moorhead is at the Social Service building to get set up with food stamps, AFDC, general assistance, housing and medical assistance." The writer added that "on numerous occasions, migrants deliver babies in our community hospitals which taxpayers and hospitals end up paying for." Despite its popularity, the argument that Mexicans were coming to take advantage of the state's welfare system was soundly refuted by a 1992 study published by the Urban Coalition and Sin Fronteras. It calculated that immigrants from Mexico and elsewhere in Latin America paid far more in taxes than they received in return from refunds and tax-based services.[52] Contrary to popular perceptions and media portrayals, Mexican immigrants in Minnesota supported a social-services system from which they received proportionally few benefits.

Network-based interpretations suggest that once a small number of immigrants establish themselves permanently, they induce further settlement by attracting family members and close acquaintances. A newspaper reporter used a network theory to explain the phenomenal growth of the Mexican population of Oslo, a town of 362 people in 1990, where the population increased from 1% to 17% in the previous decade, mostly after 1987 when many began purchasing houses and mobile homes. The unofficial "Mexican mayor" of town, Roy Martínez, spearheaded the influx, welcoming new families and helping them settle, for almost half of them were his relatives.[53] While the case of Oslo suggests they exist, the popular application of network accounts typically fails to explain why, when, and where settlement takes place. Mexicans came to many small towns and cities in Minnesota as seasonal, migrant, and temporary workers for several generations before they began settling in large numbers. They had long used networks to obtain employment, but relatively few settled outside of the Twin Cities until the late 20th century. Why did they fail to settle for so long? Network interpretations also do not explain comparative behavior, or why in many Great Lakes states migrants who worked in the same agricultural industries settled much earlier and in greater numbers than in Minnesota. Network models cannot account for why Minnesota's slower settlement in earlier years reversed so quickly during the 1990s. Networks operate, but as the case of Minnesota suggests, other conditions are necessary for widespread settlement to occur.

A final explanation, the role of economic changes and their political implications, concentrates on the longstanding reality that Mexicans came to Minnesota primarily in search of work. Yet economic cycles are difficult to predict, and at the beginning of the most recent one many observers expected the Midwest to experience an economic decline. In industrialized agriculture, prognosticators became obsessed with mechanization, a term they often used as a code word for job loss. Simultaneously, they often accepted without criticism a notion that the economy of the United States was shifting inevitably from an industrial to service-centered base.

The predictions obscured economic complexities that occurred in the subsequent generation. Many industries declined sharply, but others did not, while several sectors of the economy expanded or were restructured, particularly service industries. The cumulative impact was that employer demands for Mexicans accelerated sharply, resulting in an unprecedented growth of long-established barrios and the appearance of many Mexican neighborhoods in small towns, big cities, and many working-class suburbs.

The Rural World

Seasonal employment expanded during the 1960s and 1970s in prominent cannery operations including Owatonna Canning; Green Giant; Libby, McNeill and Libby; Joan of Arc; and Stokeley Van Camp. The companies, which produced canned corn, peas, squash, asparagus, and other vegetables, had long hired Mexican workers in the fields but were now luring them directly into the plants.[54] At Owatonna Canning in the mid-1970s, more than 1,175 seasonal workers found jobs in the fields picking asparagus and other crops and in the cannery. In Rochester, Seneca Foods and other canneries hired hundreds of seasonal workers from Texas. The state's cannery operations became part of major transnational food corporations but continued to pay seasonal workers minimum wages under difficult working conditions. At Owatonna Canning, it was reported that the "noise from the machines in the plant is deafening," the "pace is furious," and the "work is unpleasant." Many employers provided housing on their own properties, where seasonal workers resided in crowded conditions in trailer barracks with little privacy, and at times even spouses were not permitted to live together. The companies also arranged for camp housing in nearby towns or outside the city limits, where housing regulations were fewer and less strictly enforced. The more stable employment of cannery work contributed to settling out in the early 1970s.[55]

Many employers claimed that migrants returned to Minnesota every year because conditions in the state were exceptionally good, but families who came to the state had different stories to tell. Francisco Reyes and his family members first came to Minnesota shortly after World War II and many continued to migrate into the mid-1980s. He recalled frequent cases of mistreatment by employers, including one instance when a grower placed thirteen family

Workers at the Green Giant canning factory near Le Sueur, 1950–55. The work was grueling while it lasted, which was only until the crops had been picked and processed.

members on a single time card in order to avoid paying the legal minimum wage. Despite the difficult conditions, Mexican foods and conjunto music permeated workers' camps, and recreational centers spread into the neighboring communities as agricultural workers found opportunities to establish roots.

Settling out received a boost from federal programs created during the 1960s and 1970s aimed directly at migrant worker education, training, and settlement. As fewer growers were providing housing, workers were compelled to find places for themselves in nearby towns where they had to sign longer leases, increasing the likelihood of remaining once the season ended. In 1976, Migrants in Action concluded that between 10,000 and 18,000 migrants came to Minnesota annually, of whom at least 2,000 would settle in different parts of the state. By 2003, an estimated 15,000 to 25,000 migrants arrived in the state each year, the majority employed in the sugar-beet fields, and thousands of them opted to remain after the season ended.[56]

More important than either agricultural or cannery employment in Minnesota was meat-packing, an industry that had played a critical role in the initial formation of St. Paul's West Side barrio. Within the context of nationwide trends from the late 1970s through the 1990s, packinghouses moved out of Chicago, St. Paul, Omaha, and the Kansas Cities to small towns on the plains and the prairies to lower costs while they created new products and marketing techniques. The shift was part of corporate restructuring, moving processing plants closer to the point of production of beef, pork, chicken, and turkey products.

The turkey-processing industry was a particularly notable case for Minnesota. Prior to the 1960s, the industry had been primarily a seasonal operation providing whole birds for the Thanksgiving and Christmas holidays. To gain a larger market share, producers promoted turkey as more wholesome than beef or pork. National per capita turkey consumption increased by 78% from 1980 to 1990. By 1993 Minnesota had 112 turkey plants employing more than 7,000 workers, mostly Mexicans. In 2004 Minnesota led the nation in turkey production.[57]

A critical feature of corporate restructuring involved reducing worker autonomy, paying lower wages, and offering fewer benefits in order to increase profits. Wages in meat-packing had averaged almost $11.00 per hour in plants during the late 1970s. By 1990, employers had reduced entry-level wages to around $6.00 or slightly higher, sped up the production line, and created working conditions that were more dangerous and less healthful than before.

Employers turned primarily to Chicanos and Mexican immigrants, augmented by smaller numbers of workers from Southeast Asia and Africa. Willmar in 2000 had the largest concentration of Mexicans outside the Twin Cities, most working at the Jennie-O turkey plant.

According to a number of studies, because of low wages and dangerous working conditions, the new plants had phenomenal rates of employee turnover, at times exceeding 100% annually. The corporate employers often spent large sums to attract workers. To reduce those costs, they encouraged workers to develop a less formal recruitment network that they hoped would become self-perpetuating. In the winter and early spring, they contacted employees from the previous season, encouraging them to use their own contacts and word-of-mouth recruitment and sometimes even paid them special bonuses to spread the word that employment was available. Employers also used radio and newspaper advertisements and private employment agencies along the border in South Texas, where the message of work extended into the Mexican interior.[58] The networks inducing the greatest settlement of Mexicans in Minnesota were not inspired by workers, but by direct employer initiative.

In justifying the company need to recruit workers from long distances, spokesmen like Raoul Baxter of John Morrell asserted that "The meatpacking industry is one of the last in the country where people with basically no marketable skills have a chance to make a decent income" of $8.00 to $9.00 per hour plus benefits. Baxter added, "That's opportunity."[59]

Scores of Mexican neighborhoods appeared in small communities, including Madelia, Marshall, Worthington, Willmar, and Litchfield. The impact on small towns was substantial. In the early 1990s, the Montfort plant in Worthington employed 1,400 workers, while Heartland Foods in Marshall had 600, and Tony Downs in St. James had 500. Not surprisingly, according to the 2000 census, the towns where packing operations had expanded had the highest proportion of Mexicans in the state, with St. James approaching 25%, Worthington 20%, and Willmar 16%.[60]

In Madelia, a rapid surge in the Mexican population took place as a result of a Downs decision to increase production there in 1989 by adding a second shift and to recruit and bus workers directly from South Texas. The impact was immediate, as the 1980 census reported that Madelia had fewer than 100 Latinos, while by 1990 the number rose to 198, including nearly 60% of the 280 plant workers. Within two years the number of plant employees had doubled again, most recruited by the company from Brownsville, McAllen, and other cities and towns along the Rio Grande.[61] The company used advertisements in English and Spanish to lure workers with promises of a steady job and decent housing.

Downs set up two housing clusters on its own properties for new arrivals. One was the "Bird Cage Motel" located directly behind the factory, "a fly-infested garage that doubles as a kitchen." The second was a complex of about three dozen mobile home units located on the eastern edge of town. Not unexpectedly, when workers had the opportunity, they moved out of company housing to rent or purchase inexpensive dwellings in and near town. By 1992, an estimated 25% of Madelia's 2,200 residents were Latinos. The network the company established permitted a regular influx of new workers. Downs hired both United States citizens of Mexican origin and Mexican citizens, and according to an estimate in 1993, between 10 and 25% of its employees entered the country without proper documentation.[62] Legal assistant José Torres of Texas Rural Legal Aid asserted that Downs played undocumented Mexican workers, legal residents, and United States citizens off against each other in order to keep them divided and quiet.

In Worthington, Mexican workers were recruited to the Montfort pork plant, formerly Swift, which completed a massive plant expansion in 1989, adding 650 jobs to its slaughterhouse and more than doubling its work force, which became mostly Mexican during the 1990s. In its early efforts to attract and retain workers, the company offered a week of motel lodging and meals without charge, plus a $250.00 bonus for those who remained six months. There were only a handful of permanent Mexican residents in Worthington in the late 1980s, but by 1993 the city of 10,000 had more than 500. By the end of the decade a majority of its elementary school students were of Mexican origin.[63]

Urban Barrios

Assertions that the United States was turning into a service economy in the late 20th century generated debate, but there is no dispute that Mexican employment increased sharply in several midwestern service industries. Job losses in urban manufacturing were more than offset by gains in service industries and in smaller plants and shops.

Mexicans found jobs in several sectors where they had been insignificant a generation earlier, particularly in large hotel chains, restaurants, nurseries and landscaping, and custodial and cleaning services. Employers often claimed that they had to turn to Mexicans because European Americans and African Americans were no longer interested in such work.[64] Minnesotans often accepted such explanations without engaging in further systematic examination of employers' newfound enchantment with Mexican workers. As in the case of rural poultry and meat-packing, urban employers' restructuring of work initiated the change, as it involved wage reductions, demands for higher output, and reduced safety measures that resulted in more dangerous and less healthful conditions, offering few incentives for longer established local residents. Simultaneously, employers attacked the unions' ability to protect workers. Finally, a sharp expansion of production generated a marked increase in employer demands for workers.

The impact of the new employment was visible geographically, as Twin Cities' Mexican neighborhoods expanded phenomenally. Established barrios became more densely populated, and Mexicans moved into neighboring districts and areas where they had been insignificant earlier. Mexican neighborhoods also appeared in several suburban locations, including Shakopee, Crystal, Chaska, and New Hope, often because of the lure of jobs from specific employers. In Bloomington new jobs were available at the Mall of America. The Immigration and Naturalization Service reported that more than 1,500 undocumented workers were employed at the mall in mid-1999, compared with a mere handful two years earlier.[65]

In St. Paul, the barrio on the West Side, centering on Concord Street, renamed by business interests in 2001 as the District del Sol, expanded rapidly. Mexican families spread into adjacent neighborhoods and nearby suburbs, including West St. Paul, South St. Paul, and Inver Grove Heights. A Mexican neighborhood also appeared on the East Side of St. Paul and became the fastest growing Latino community in the city, having an estimated population of

Children took part in a Posada in St. Paul at Christmastime in 1971. They carry a tableau with small figures of Mary and Joseph, and at each house they visit they ask for shelter for the holy couple. Once the request has been granted, then the festivities begin.

14,000 in 2004. Its business district on Payne Avenue was anchored by the Plaza Latina, patterned after the Mercado Central in Minneapolis, where a range of shops catered to customers in the neighborhood.[66]

An even more impressive growth took place in Minneapolis, whose Mexican population of 29,175 in 2000 surpassed the 22,715 of St. Paul. Early in the 1990s a neighborhood composed largely of Mexican immigrants appeared in South Minneapolis, centered along Lake Street and Nicollet Avenues, and it quickly became the largest barrio in the state. By the end of the century, districts along Lake Street

Children in biblical and Mexican dress took part in a Christmas Eve Mass at Our Lady of Guadalupe Church in 1971.

housed half the city's entire Latino population, overwhelmingly of Mexican background. Several established neighborhoods exceeded 25% Latino, including Phillips, Whittier, Powderhorn Park, and Corcoran. In the mid-1990s another Mexican neighborhood appeared in Northeast Minneapolis, centered along Central Avenue and Lowry.[67]

The phenomenal increase in the Mexican population in the Twin Cities and smaller towns was the most notable demographic feature of late 20th-century Minnesota. It was unforeseen even by planners and demographers, and in 1999 the Census Bureau underestimated the Mexican population of the state by more than 50%. Even official figures made a significant undercount, according to Hispanic Advocacy and Community Empowerment Through Research (HACER), which calculated that at least 48,000

In 1965 La Casa Coronado Restaurant supplied tamales and burritos for a cart at the Minneapolis Aquatennial, which had a Latin American theme that year.

uncounted, undocumented immigrants were also employed in the local economy. The research group estimated that Mexicans comprised 30% of the state's work force in roofing and repairs; 25% in nurseries, landscaping, raising fruits and vegetables, the hotel and lodging industry, and janitorial services; and 15% of the workers in meat- and poultry-processing plants, bars, and restaurants. Mexican immigrants made a strong and positive contribution to the economy through state, municipal, and Social Security taxes, while creating thousands of jobs for other Minnesotans, contrary to the charges of many uninformed critics. As Art Rolnick, the research director of the Federal Reserve Bank in Minneapolis, acknowledged, "These workers are adding to our economic growth."[68]

Mexicans also played a critical role in the demographic recovery of the Twin Cities during the 1990s. According to the 2000 census, both St. Paul and Minneapolis increased by more than 30,000 people during the decade, reversing a 50-year decline. But as white flight continued, both cities would have lost population except for the influx of Mexicans. The Latino population grew from 53,885 to 143,382, excluding the undercount of nearly 50,000 undocumented workers as calculated by HACER.[69] The census undercounts were particularly notable in a number of smaller Minnesota communities. Based on estimates from the Minnesota State Demographic Center, the Latino population in 2004 was around 175,000 people, excluding the estimated thousands of people without documents.

At the turn of the 21st century, Minnesota's media focused on a number of general issues pertaining to Mexicans, of which the new business class, migrants, housing, social services, schools, and the police attracted its greatest attention. In keeping with the times, it was most positive in addressing the appearance of a self-conscious class of entrepreneurs, which it portrayed as the realization of the American Dream for Mexicans. It was upbeat in discussing organizing efforts by the Hispanic Chamber of Commerce of Minnesota, which sought to reinvigorate the defunct Minnesota Hispanic Chamber of Commerce by bringing both entrepreneurs and professionals into the organization. Entrepreneurial efforts increased sharply in Minnesota, as the number of Latino businesses doubled to more than 3,000 between 1990 and 2000. While impressive in absolute numbers, its growth lagged far behind the rate of Latino population increase during the period.[70]

Many of the new businesses were dependent on a Spanish-speaking clientele, promoting and selling goods and services and, in the case of national holidays, Mexican culture. Business districts expanded rapidly in the heart of the largest Mexican neighborhoods. In South Minneapolis the Mercado Central appeared, a cooperative business venture involving Mexicans and Central Americans who established *panaderías*, *pastelerías*, restaurants and other food shops and stalls, and boutiques selling clothing, crafts, and fresh products for the preparation of food, and providing other services catering directly to the Latino community. The commercial Spanish-language media also expanded rapidly, along with a number of small Spanish-language newspapers, and in 2000, the state's first full-time Spanish-language radio station began broadcasting.[71] Merchants promoted, celebrated, and in some cases fought for control over increasingly visible and commercialized Mexican holidays, contributing to a surge of popular interest in the Dieciseis de Septiembre (Independence Day) and Cinco de Mayo (Battle of Puebla).

Cultural Expressions and Tension

While Mexican businesses had only recently attracted media attention, migrant workers were a stable of media reporting. When schools established facilities for the children of seasonal agricultural workers as required by the law, many

Mexican Music

Contemporary Mexican music has strong roots in Mexican culture. Many families brought their traditions of folk and dance music with them on their trips to Minnesota. Some musicians in the 1940s and 1950s made the circuit of the migrant camps, playing for dances on weekends.

Luís Garzón, the traveling orchestra member who became the first known Mexican settler in Minnesota, opened a grocery store and put together his own orchestra in the 1920s, which played for family and community occasions. Other groups, usually playing a variety of stringed instruments, soon appeared and found the Neighborhood House and the pavilion at Harriet Island frequent venues for dances. Groups also played at celebrations like Independence Day on September 16.

By the 1940s, young people began to mix Mexican and American music, often infused with music from Mexico and the Caribbean. One musician who emerged at this time was Agusto (Augie) García, a band leader, singer, and guitar player, whose group by the late 1940s played at restaurants, for church events, and soon appeared on television.

The 1960s brought more changes to the West Side local music scene. The clearing of the flats forced people to move to the neighborhood on Concord St. or elsewhere in the Twin Cities, and the arrival of rock and roll engendered new forms of music. Augie García adapted quickly and began singing in English, earning the nickname of the "Richie Valens of the West Side." García continued to lead a band over the next two decades and in 1996 held a reunion concert at the Prom ballroom in St. Paul. Music was central to him and to the life of the community in weddings and other family gatherings, patriotic occasions like Cinco de Mayo, and religious events such as the Dia de la Virgen de Guadalupe.

Augie García along with Manuel Maurico and John Ramierz performed live on the Arle Haberle show on WTCN-TV in 1947.

adopted policies separating Mexican and European American children. Newspaper reporter Brian Anderson observed in the early 1970s that "an invisible barrier" existed between migrants and permanent residents in small towns throughout Minnesota. Later in the decade, reporter Lori Thorkelson found that when migrant workers and their families entered stores, parks, and restaurants, "there is very little intermingling of the two cultural groups."[72]

Migrant education gained considerable attention as government-sponsored programs sought to ensure that children attended classes. By 1975 more than 4,300 migrant children participated in migrant programs in 17 school districts in the state. Openly advocating one-way assimilation, the programs had few goals other than making sure that children stayed out of the fields and improved reading scores. Oslo band teacher, Don Flaagen, was more explicit, suggesting that the main purpose of summer programs was "to get them used to our culture. As far as I'm concerned, these people are getting their Spanish culture at their regular schools in Texas." School authorities and growers had little appreciation for the development of independent thinking or autonomy among migrant children.[73]

Within local communities, officials and authorities openly tolerated discrimination against migrants. Louis Martínez, who was a migrant worker before settling in the Red River Valley, observed in 1969 that, "prices go up in this area when the migrants come in. . . . There is one guy in East Grand Forks who spends all Saturday night in his store marking up prices for the migrants who come in on Sunday." Similar stories were repeated in rural communities with large influxes of migrant workers. At the end of the century, tensions accelerated because many locals continued to assume that all Mexicans could be mistreated. Alfred Alres, attorney for Southern Minnesota Regional Legal Services, stated: "I don't think the [Freeborn] County Board knows the definition of 'migrant worker,'" an indication of its members' inability to distinguish between migrants and permanent residents.[74]

Confusion between migrants and settlers was perhaps unavoidable when the sudden and massive migration for permanent settlement accelerated in the 1980s, upsetting longstanding rural rhythms and expectations by longer-established residents that Mexicans would depart in the fall. Individuals in power had difficulty accepting the changes, including the Freeborn County Commissioner who urged that local officials travel to Texas and inform Mexicans there were no jobs available, without success. While unable to prevent them from settling in the state, many landlords and realtors reverted to unwritten restrictive housing practices, which explain in part why Mexican colonias and barrios appeared. State representative Marv Dauner noted that in the Detroit Lakes area, site of a Swift-Eckrich packing plant, "property owners are reluctant to house migrant families," in violation of the law. Crookston police officer Glen Torgerson observed that, "Local people find ways not to house the migrants" by charging double or triple damage deposits, compelling them to sign long leases, and using answering machines to screen people's non-Minnesota accents. Some owners imposed apartment showing fees, employment verification, credit checks, and written references, none of which ensured tenancy. In many instances landlords took apartments off the market when Mexicans sought to rent them, using a number of false pretexts, including that they had just been rented or that they needed renovation. When individuals were able to rent units, landlords often imposed harsh rules on Mexican tenants that other renters did not experience. Project Advocacy's Raquel Ybarra noted, "You can't believe how fast the rules change" when Mexican workers sought housing.[75]

In many small towns, European Americans tried to treat their new neighbors as they had earlier treated migrants. Willmar Mayor F. J. Reynolds said he frequently heard older residents of his city say that they "should go back to Texas, where they came from" and other things about Mexicans that were "unprintable." Established European American residents regularly confused migrants with settlers, the common denominator in their minds being Mexican background and appearance. One European American resident complained, "migrant workers come up from Texas and use the parks and recreation areas without paying taxes." In East Grand Forks flyers were spread throughout a Mexican section of town with messages reading, "Go back to Mexico, you welfare grease-balls." A Madelia resident and member of the American Legion asserted, "financially-wise, they're not doing us any good. . . . I'm sure they're an asset to the liquor store." A former farm worker who settled in Moorhead in 1989 responded, "People tell us, 'Go back to Mexico.' But it's not our intention to run away from here. This is our home. We're here, and we're going to stay."[76]

Local media spent a great deal of attention on the settling process and conflicts that arose in small towns that had long been ethnically homogeneous and stable. Old timers often expected that they could treat Mexican permanent residents as they had long treated migrants. Willmar resident Glynda Gámez stated that, "in the grocery store, people look at you like you're going to steal something." In 1971, Alice Méndez, age 21, who lived in Crookston most of her life, stated, "We're used to going uptown and watching people stare at us. It doesn't bother us." One Texas-born Rochester man complained in the early 1990s that pellets from a shotgun damaged siding on his home, trucks ripped up his lawn, and white supremacist literature appeared on his doorstep. At work he had to tolerate racist jokes and denigrating names, including being addressed as spic and "taco bender."[77]

Tension in Blooming Prairie centered on a trailer park inhabited mostly by Mexicans. Long-established residents complained in newspapers and public hearings, while asserting that despite a lack of violence, "that does not mean all is well." Frank Treviño was born and lived in Blooming Prairie until age 15 when he moved to Texas, where he lived several more years, married, and had children. Later he moved back to Blooming Prairie with his family and made a startling discovery: "It surprised me that so many people are so bitter. When my kids started school here they said, 'Man, these people are *prejudiced*.' There's more racism in Blooming Prairie now than there was in the 1950s." The Blooming Prairie superintendent of schools acknowledged, European American "kids come to school with negative attitudes toward Hispanics. They call them dirtballs and that kind of stuff."[78]

Many concerns were addressed publicly as a result of investigations by the Minnesota Human Rights Department in the mid-1990s that uncovered only a miniscule portion of actual cases, as the Spanish Speaking Affairs Council reported, because "many violations go unreported for fear of reprisal either through job loss or inability to obtain housing." In its investigation, the Minnesota House of Representatives Housing Committee concluded that in rural sections of the state Mexicans "face overwhelming barriers to finding housing."[79]

The media also addressed the availability of social services and the stereotype of welfare loafer, which was much more pervasive than that of Mexican as entrepreneur. The widespread self-perception of the North Star State as welcoming provides an insight into social relations, a newspaper reporter was surprised to discover when he visited Crystal City, Texas, where "tales of discrimination against migrants in Minnesota abound." One of the few serious investigative reports on the issue concluded that public animosity toward migrant and non-migrant Mexican workers' use of public assistance was based on several misconceptions related to the nature of migrant farm work, and how public assistance programs operated, as well as racial and cultural biases. Hostility toward migrants' use of emergency public assistance typically addressed it as a drain on local service resources, while the report noted that starting in 1991 the funds were provided 50% by federal government and 50% by the state, none by the county. Yet local government officials, including a retired Albert Lea school administrator, complained, "We cannot continue to fund families that come to Minnesota for the good life."[80]

The supervisor of the Minnesota Human Rights Department (HRD) reported that county welfare workers frequently told clients on first arriving at their offices, "Why don't you go back to Texas?" The HRD also described a case in which officials of the Polk County Community Social Services Department convinced a United States woman of Mexican origin to turn in her undocumented husband for deportation as a condition for obtaining food stamps for their hungry children. It found that "they intimidated her into believing she would lose her food stamp eligibility." A critic observed of administrative and political actors in Clay County, "They appear hostile, prejudiced, sometimes making shooting-from-the-hip decisions." A 1993 Minnesota Department of Human Services investigation of Clay County welfare applications revealed widespread discrimination, as more than one-fourth of requests for food stamps were improperly handled, and a high proportion of clients were wrongly suspended or their payments were reduced or terminated.[81]

Meanwhile, in 1993 legislators from areas with high concentrations of Mexicans, including Republican Representative Kevin Goodno of Moorhead and Republican State Senator Dean Anderson of Willmar, led efforts to curb welfare. Goodno claimed that the proposed legislation would "remove lawbreakers from welfare rolls." Anderson, referring to recent arrivals from Mexico, defended the measures on the grounds that Minnesota had become a "welfare magnet," despite evidence to the contrary. Their efforts culminated in legislation that cut benefits to immigrants without proper documentation from General Assistance, Medical Assistance, and the Work Readiness Program.[82]

For those European Americans who befriended or conducted business with Mexicans, difficulties occasionally ensued. In Heron Lake, local residents boycotted an Anglo-American businessman who rented a house to a Mexican family, threw eggs at family members, and knocked his wife unconscious with a rock thrown behind their store. Furthermore, a mobile home they rented out was burned down the day after they received an anonymous phone call warning them of the impending arson. Heron Lake resident Cipriano Peña noted, "There's a lot of prejudice here. We never dealt with this kind of thing in Texas. I don't know how to deal with it. But there's a lot of friendly people in town, a lot of nice people."[83]

While obtaining their own housing often led to serious problems, the alternative of company housing was much less attractive. In Madelia in the early 1990s, Tony Downs provided "ramshackle housing" as a "service" for $25.00 per week. Following years of complaints about abuses at Downs, the *Minneapolis Star Tribune* carried out an investigative report in 1992. As a result of the bad publicity and threats of a public probe, Downs hired workers the following day to clean up the units, picking up garbage, mowing lawns, and painting and installing screens. But the publicity compelled the Minnesota Department of Labor and Industry to conduct the probe nevertheless, which was completed less than three weeks after the *Star Tribune* report. The hasty inspection determined that Downs had not adequately cleaned up and repaired the company units. The department found 41 health and safety violations, several of which posed a danger of injury and possible death to inhabitants, and it fined Tony Downs $17,200.[84]

Mexicans who sought to establish permanent roots

and purchase houses faced different obstacles. A study completed in 2000 found that they were more than twice as likely as other Minnesotans to accept higher-cost, subprime mortgages when buying their homes, often from predatory lenders. They were trapped into accepting unfavorable loans according to a 2002 study by the Association of Community Organizations for Reform Now (ACORN), which reported that Latinos and blacks were about three times more likely to be rejected for mortgages in the metropolitan Twin Cities area than whites. Among upper-income blacks and Latinos, the denial rate was nearly four times the rate for upper-income whites. The report found that discrimination combined with economic factors accounted for sharply different homeownership rates in Minnesota—77% for whites, 32% for blacks, and 43% for Latinos.[85]

Tensions rose and performance suffered in schools, particularly when teachers and administrators harbored negative expectations and treated students differently. Donovan Dulski, Moorhead High School principal, publicly stated that: "Because of their migratory nature, many Hispanic students don't have the background to compete educationally. . . . There are isolated cases of success." Students reported that teachers bluntly told them to "go back to Mexico." A Moorhead school employee grabbed a Chicana in the lunch line, accused her of skipping classes that morning, and stated, "That's all you Mexicans come here for—you come to eat." Despite several witnesses to the incident, the principal denied that it occurred and claimed that verifiable proof was lacking, preferring to defend rather than reprimand the abusive employee. Throughout the state, teachers and administrators branded minority students as gang members because they wore popular clothing or brand-name sports attire or simply because they associated with each other. In Moorhead, tensions grew as the number of Mexican students in the school system increased in the late 1980s and 1990s, and swastikas and

Family Foodways

Traditional Mexican food was family fare, often one-pot meals that were not highly seasoned. Sopa was noodles or rice in broth, and caldo was a meat and vegetable stew. Menudo was a soup with tripe as the main ingredient. All were served with tortillas, which were usually made of corn and less often of wheat. Beans, especially pinto beans, were a staple. Leftovers could be mashed and fried as refritos. Rice was a frequent part of the meal. It was stir fried before the broth was added. Mexican chocolate was the basis of mole, a sauce served over chicken or other meat.

Settled out families often raised their own vegetables because many favorite ingredients were not available in Minnesota stores. Residents on St. Paul's West Side grew chiles and tomatillos. As late as the 1940s, cooks could not find cilantro, cumin, chile ancho, or Mexican chocolate in local stores. Such foods had to be brought or shipped in from Texas or Mexico. By the 1960s, these foods had begun to appear in Twin Cities markets but not yet in other parts of Minnesota. A restaurant owner in Owatonna had to make trips to Minneapolis or St. Paul to find supplies.

As lifestyles changed, so did foodways. By the late 20th century, many families no longer had the time to make many traditional dishes, which then became part of special occasion meals, such as at Christmas or for weddings and birthdays. This was especially true of tamales, which often take a day to prepare. First the corn kernels had to be boiled to remove the hulls, then the corn was ground to make a paste. The corn husks for wrapping the tamales had to be stripped from the corn cobs, washed, and dried; the meat needed to be cooked and shredded; and a sauce of chile, garlic, and salt prepared. Then came the assembly. The corn paste was spread on the husk, and a layer of meat and sauce came next. The husk was folded to cover the filling, and the tamales steamed over a pan of hot water. Nowadays cooks can save a few steps by buying cornmeal and cleaned and dried corn husks, but it is still a time-consuming process to make tamales.

Mrs. Julio López and Mrs. Francisco Rangel prepared tamales at Our Lady of Guadalupe for Independence Day festivities in 1958.

racial slurs appeared on school lockers. Moorhead school administrators engaged in additional forms of disparate treatment, including ordering minority students to pick up trash along the roadside, denying children of migrant workers the opportunity to register late, and permitting hall monitors to assign detention to Mexican students while not punishing white students for the same actions. In St. James, the coordinator of adult education acknowledged rising tensions in schools but justified it with a claim that, "This is a language problem, not a race problem."[86]

Disparate treatment contributed to poor school performance and high dropout rates among Mexican students in Minnesota. There were sharp differences in basic skills tests at all levels in math, English, and general writing. In 2002, statewide passing rates in the tests for 10th graders were 94% for whites, 81% for American Indians, 79% for Asians, 70% for Latinos, and 62% for African Americans. Meanwhile, graduation rates for Latino students who entered high school in 1997 after four years was only 47%, compared with 78% for Minnesotans overall. In Minneapolis the community initiated a number of creative efforts to provide education for Mexican students, including two after-school programs, La Escuelita and the San Miguel Middle School, a tuition-free institution run by the Christian Brothers that opened in 2000 in the Phillips neighborhood.[87]

A final subject that attracted widespread media attention, Mexicans and law enforcement, further unveiled how agencies manipulated institutional racism against Mexicans, often using pretexts such as the so-called wars on crime and drugs or the "illegal alien" problem. Discrimination and abuse by police forces were well documented, as was criticism by Mexicans of those police officers who gained notoriety for improper behavior and belligerent and profane language. Apart from the extraordinary cases, Mexicans were stopped, searched and frisked, and fined at disproportionate rates. A study completed in 2001 found that St. Paul police searched black and Latino motorists at about twice the rate (19.6% and 16.7%) as Asian American and white drivers (9.2% and 8.5% respectively).[88]

Throughout Minnesota, Mexicans had grievances about local police. When East Grand Forks residents complained that racist literature was being distributed in their neighborhood, the police not only failed to respond, they later claimed they did not recall the incident. In Worthington, Latino residents expressed anger over unfair treatment toward people of Mexican appearance, with police stopping them simply to verify identification, even following people to their homes to check their residences for undocumented individuals. In one case, David Sifuentes, born and reared in San Antonio and a four-year resident of Worthington, reported that when he was stopped on the street by police and asked for his green card, he explained that he was a citizen. But police officers insisted that, "He had to have a green card because he was Hispanic." He retorted, "I've never had this problem. My color says I'm illegal. But I'm an American citizen."[89]

In Willmar, relations reached a boiling point as Mexicans complained of heavy-handed treatment and racist and sexist language by Anglo officers. Even Willmar Police Chief Todd Miller acknowledged that there was "prejudice involved" in law enforcement officers' actions. Mexican residents were also frustrated that police were less willing to protect them or deal with complaints they filed. Newspaper reporter Richard Meryhew found that European Americans in Willmar considered relations with police good, but Mexicans widely perceived them as unsatisfactory. In an effort to improve relations, police and sheriffs deputies took a course in Spanish, both to enhance cultural understanding and to make possible communication with all the residents of the community.[90]

Many Mexicans faced an even more uncertain life when they were subjected to the Immigration and Naturaliza-

A Mexican Police Officer

To address the problem of racism in Willmar, Police Chief Todd Miller hired a Mexican police officer to conduct business and to smooth relations between the police and the local community. In 1990 the city hired Arturo Dearo, a bilingual policeman of Mexican origin. City officials perhaps hoped that Dearo would not offend Willmar police officers, as he had blond hair and blue eyes. Furthermore as Dearo's former supervisor, Captain Coy Clanton of the Texas State Highway Patrol in Midland, observed, "I did not perceive him to be an overly sensitive person about his race."

Dearo, however, quickly faced problems, not from the community but from his fellow officers. He was warned to watch his back when he insisted on equal treatment. He was called a "dirty Mexican" and falsely accused by other police officers of selling drugs and taking bribes. Shortly afterward a racist flyer was posted at police headquarters entitled "A Challenge to White Citizens," which described Hispanics as "mongrels," "parasites," "thugs," "muggers," and "drug lords" who impregnate "our white daughters." In an effort to soothe relations, police officers were required to attend a 12-hour cultural diversity program in the spring of 1992. Nevertheless, harassment against Dearo continued, and he filed a lawsuit in the United States District Court in July 1992 for harassment based on ethnicity. In September, he found a hand grenade with the pin half-pulled in his car, although it turned out to be a non-explosive dummy. A supposedly "independent" police probe of the incident concluded that the grenade had been placed there by "accident." Meanwhile, the police chief asserted that Dearo's fears were "unfounded," and the attorney defending the city claimed that these were "isolated incidents." The case was settled out of court, and in late 1992 Dearo moved to St. Paul where the police department hired him as an officer. He was not embittered by his experience in Willmar and even defended his decision to move to Minnesota, stating, "We like it here, even though it's a little cold. We think it's a good place to raise your family." Despite his unpleasant experience with institutional racism, he found enough that was positive to remain in the state.

tion Service, whose raids against undocumented persons were dutifully reported by the media. The agency attributed its increased activity to the upsurge in the number of undocumented workers settling in the state. Roy Garza of the Spanish Speaking Affairs Council pointed out the discriminatory nature of the action; more than 95% were directed against Mexicans, who formed less than a quarter of the undocumented population of the state, most of whom were Europeans and Canadians.[91]

The most spectacular INS operations sought out Mexican workers in food-processing plants. In Marshall in 1992, the INS staged a number of highly publicized raids on Heartland Foods' turkey-processing operations. Local police instigated the searches by calling INS officials to report that they had seen forged green cards. The raids also had a negative impact on workers' collective morale and organizational efforts, preventing them from taking collective action against their employer.[92]

The media also reported efforts aimed at establishing an institutional presence to deal with Mexicans in Minnesota. The most popular included organizations based in the community, churches, social and cultural clubs, and labor groups.

Community-based committees appeared in many places when city leaders expressed concern about problems stemming from rapid change and the influx of new residents. The officials tended to control these organizations although Mexicans often participated. In Willmar, a minority advisory committee was created to deal with social and economic problems "caused by the rapid increase in Hispanics." In Crookston, city leaders were concerned that the influx of Mexicans in the area "has had a series of consequences that has affected the whole fabric of life in the city," and in 1987 it formed the Social Concerns Committee composed of public officials, growers, housing owners, church groups, law enforcement, and migrant representatives. Their major goal was to establish effective communication and "destroy the negative impact of unfounded rumors." In Blooming Prairie, long-established residents became "embroiled in a not-so-private debate over a new wave of Hispanic families moving into the city." During public hearings in 1987, they leveled complaints that the city had "become the welfare capital of Steele County." As a result of the tension, in 1988 the Blooming Prairie Center, Incorporated, opened as a meeting place for the Latino Community, leading to accusations of reverse racism, as one resident said bitterly, because, "We ain't got a place for the white kids to go to."[93]

In Madelia, local authorities established the Watonwan

County Multicultural Integration Project, which sought to address such issues as the lack of affordable housing, labor shortages, inadequate child care, need for a bilingual peace officer, and relevant aspects of the criminal justice system.[94] However many of the leaders of the organizations created to deal with another generation of "the Mexican Problem," were insensitive and unwilling to understand the need for change.

Another type of collective activity, sports, variously served political, cultural, and social functions. Some activities had earlier roots, including Club Azteca in Albert Lea that local Mexican residents had formed in 1949. It later became the core of a chapter of the League of United Latin American Citizens (LULAC) and a stimulus to other activities in the area for many decades. While some Worthington residents concerned about politics and the treatment of workers founded their own Hispanic Organization in 1992, a larger number became involved in sports. Several teams formed the Worthington Baseball League, comprised primarily of immigrants who came to work in the meat-packing plants.[95]

In Willmar, the Hispanic Alliance appeared in 1992, with a mission of creating opportunities for Latinos and serving as a liaison between cultures. Despite its modest goals and middle-class concerns, some of the city's European Americans criticized its members for their ostensibly outspoken style and willingness to be advocates. One Willmar official even suggested the group should try to act more like the Sons of Norway and focus on keeping cultural traditions alive while refraining from a social or political agenda. Such an approach would necessarily fail to deal with difficulties that occurred when Norway's own sons in this "strong, conservative Scandinavian town" accused Mexican high school students of being gangbangers. Chicano students at nearby St. Cloud State University through Proyecto Willmar had a more direct and effective remedy, namely encouraging the

Sports—baseball, basketball, and soccer—were part of many young peoples' lives. The basketball team from Our Lady of Guadalupe Church won the American League Championship, CAA, and posed with their trophy in 1948–49.

students to organize themselves. Through Raza Unida, the high school students addressed community and school issues while they improved their grades.[96]

Mexicans organized in various work settings and engaged in a number of notable events, particularly in packing plants, where they faced constant pressure from employers and the INS. A notable collective struggle involved the employees of Heartland Foods in Marshall. They had many grievances against their employer, who engaged in a number of unscrupulous hiring practices, including permitting company personnel to take fees in exchange for jobs. Female workers encountered sexual harassment by management.

Soccer

Lalo Sánchez moved to St. Paul following service in the military police in World War II. Having played soccer as a boy in Mexico, he wanted to continue with the game. Besides playing on semiprofessional teams, he began coaching elementary and high school youth from the West Side. He soon found out that the boys knew little about soccer. Yet by 1974 his team, the Aztecas Soccer Team, were Minnesota State Champions. In 39 games, they had only seven goals scored against them while scoring 169 goals against their opponents, the most any team had scored that year.

Despite this success, Sánchez encountered obstacles. He found it difficult to obtain a sponsor for his club, he had to meet expenses out of his own pocket to pay for referees, insurance, bandages, and bags of compound for marking the field. He also ran into objections from the Minnesota Association for using boys from Mexico. The United States Soccer Federation had no ban on players who were not born in the United States, but the Minnesota Association would allow only two boys from Mexico to be on the team at any one time. Nevertheless, Sánchez could point out with pride that four of his players had gone on to play soccer professionally.

The Aztecas Soccer Club, August 1972, at Lake Calhoun, Minneapolis: front row, Ted Lozano, Salvador Lozano, ? Romo, Jesus Romo, Pepe Orteja, Rafael Romo, Arturo Romo, Rudy Grazia; back row, Tobey Columga, Marty Moreno, Alex Verdeja, Peter Zarat (?), (?), Lenny Sanchez, Richard Van den Bosch, Ginó Falores

A more notorious abuse involved the company calling in the INS to stage raids to remove undocumented workers, curiously timed at six-month intervals, immediately before workers were scheduled to receive their semiannual bonuses. The practice permitted the company to avoid paying hundreds of thousands of dollars in earnings due workers. Although the INS fined the company for hiring undocumented workers, the penalty was less than half the amount it

---

Organizing a Union Local

In a significant labor struggle, Mexican immigrant women led an organizing drive at the Holiday Inn Express of Minneapolis. In 1997, Rosa Albino got a job at the hotel, and she soon assisted a brother and four sisters in obtaining employment there as well. Earlier one of them had worked at another Twin Cities hotel organized by the Hotel Employees and Restaurant Employees Industrial Union (HERE), Local 17. The Spanish-speaking staff of the local had organized hundreds of immigrants who cleaned hotels and office buildings and worked in restaurants.

The Albinos, because of their union experience, knew they could protest disparate treatment by management. Other workers were allowed 40 minutes to clean a room; received morning, afternoon, and lunch breaks; were guaranteed pay raises after 90 days and again after one year; and worked full eight-hour days. The Mexicans were permitted only 20 minutes to clean a room, received no breaks or pay raises, and often worked short shifts. These management policies belied employer claims that they were hiring Mexican immigrants simply because they could not find enough available workers locally.

Management denial of equal treatment strengthened the workers' determination to organize. As Holiday Inn employee Norma Lerma del Toro observed, "We just wanted better treatment." The union called for an election on August 27, 1999, and won 11-7, with only four employees in the unit not voting. The Albinos formed the majority of those who voted for the union and the core of the negotiating team, which was scheduled to begin bargaining with management in early November.

Their plan was disrupted on October 13 when hotel manager Kevin Koenig called eight union members separately into his office. The unsuspecting workers were surprised to find Immigration and Naturalization Service authorities there to verify his suspicions that they were undocumented. Koenig claimed that he had received a tip that they were "illegal aliens," so he was simply performing his civic duty. The INS immediately sent two men and four women to jail because they lacked proof of legal residence in the United States, while two others, mothers with minor children, were not detained. As Reyna Albino recalled on being arrested and handcuffed, "They made us feel like criminals, like bad people, that we did something wrong when all we were doing was working." The employees acknowledged that they had committed misdemeanors and expected to be deported promptly, which had been standard policy since the 1920s.

Koenig expressly asserted that informing the INS "has nothing to do with the union." While employers were required to hire workers with proof of legal residency or citizenship, they were not

---

would otherwise have paid in bonuses. Finally, in May 1993, angry workers and family members staged a highly publicized strike in protest of the unethical company actions and forced the company to respond. The employer agreed to pay deported workers 50% of bonuses due and to release their paychecks to authorized individuals. Furthermore, once the company realized that the organized workers were willing to challenge its authority, the INS raids subsided.[97]

obligated to inform the INS if they discovered that an employee lacked proper documentation. They need only to terminate such employees. While the workers were in jail, community activists and allies staged several public demonstrations, drawing attention to the workers' plight. The demonstrations, along with critical support from Centro Legal, HERE, and Father Ed Leahy, associate pastor at Holy Rosary Catholic Church in South Minneapolis to which the Albino family belonged, resulted in the workers being released from jail after a week and not being deported.

Centro Legal filed a suit against hotel management in conjunction with the U.S. Equal Employment Opportunity Commission (EEOC) and the National Labor Relations Board (NLRB). It gained a legal victory when the labor bodies ruled on the Día de los Reyes, January 6, 2000, that Holiday Inn had violated the 1964 Civil Rights Act by discriminating against Mexicans based on national origin and that it had engaged in retaliatory firing of its employees.

Due to pressure resulting from the investigation, Holiday Inn agreed to settle with the workers out of court and thereby avoided acknowledgment of wrongdoing. While management asserted that the settlement would cost less than a legal battle, more importantly it would avoid a powerful court precedent. Holiday Inn agreed to pay $72,000—$1,000 compensatory damages and $7,000 back wages for each of the nine workers involved.

The Holiday Inn case proved significant on several levels. First, the initiative by Mexican workers permitted HERE, Local 17, to sign a union contract with management of the Minneapolis hotel in January 2000. The two-year agreement offered starting wages at $7.25 an hour for housekeepers, with guaranteed raises after 90 days and again after one year. Management also promised that it would not engage in discriminatory actions against union employees and that its managers would receive training programs. It demonstrated the significance of collective efforts by Mexican workers who were determined, "to stay in the country as long as possible and fight back."

Second, the ruling by the EEOC was a landmark, representing the first time the commission ruled in favor of undocumented workers on the issue of employer discrimination. The decision could encourage attorneys to accept cases on behalf of undocumented workers for discrimination in the work place. Yet discriminatory treatment was embedded in the decision. The NLRB and the INS have a standing agreement that the INS will not be used to stop union activity, but any immigration entry into the workplace or removal of workers sympathetic to unions during any organizational or election campaign has a chilling effect on union activity.

The media also reported efforts by churches and unions to reach out to Mexicans. The Catholic Church created the Hispanic Ministry Leadership Team in 1997 to work in the Archdiocese of St. Paul and Minneapolis, and by 2004 there were 18 parishes that offered weekly Spanish-language Masses in the archdiocese. Meanwhile, 13 parishes in the Diocese of Winona and seven in the Diocese of New Ulm also had Spanish-language ministries. The churches provided a wide range of religious programs and also worked on specific community issues, especially housing and immigration.[98]

Struggles by Mexican workers helped shake the labor movement and influence top AFL-CIO leadership to alter many longstanding exclusionary policies. In 2000, it finally demanded blanket amnesty for all undocumented immigrants, reversing its position on the 1986 Immigration Reform and Control Act supporting restrictive immigration legislation. In the Twin Cities, Service Employees International Union Local 26, representing workers in commercial buildings, had a membership at the turn of the century estimated at 40% immigrant, mostly Mexicans. There was also a large membership in the United Food and Commercial Workers, especially Local 789 in central Minnesota, whose president, Bill Pearson, "toyed with the idea of hiring a Spanish-speaking organizer" but rejected it as not being a "cost-effective move." Pearson simultaneously complained, "It just kills me when somebody says 'you don't represent us very well.'"[99] Institutional change came slowly even in unions whose survival depended on Mexican membership.

The 21st century opened much differently from the 20th for Mexicans in Minnesota, and in June 2004, President Vicente Fox of Mexico paid a visit to the state. The trip became front-page news in the Minnesota press, which highlighted the growing ties between the two countries. As a symbolic measure, Fox promised to expedite the reopening of a consulate in the Twin Cities, and community leaders announced that the consulate would open by March 2005 in the new headquarters building of Chicanos Latinos Unidos En Servicio (CLUES) on the East Side of St. Paul.[100]

Personal Account:
A West Side Family
by Ramedo and Catalina Saucedo

Ramedo and Catalina Saucedo lived, worked, and raised a family in the Mexican neighborhood of the West Side of St. Paul. Catalina was born in 1930 in Texas and moved to St. Paul in 1943. Ramedo, also born in 1930, was a native of St. Paul. Both attended schools on the West Side. After serving with the National Guard during the Korean War, Ramedo graduated from the University of Minnesota. The couple married in 1956 and had two children, a daughter born in 1961 and a son in 1964. Ramedo taught in the Minneapolis public school system and was the director of the Mexican American History Project at the Minnesota Historical Society in 1975–77. The following is an excerpt from one of the interviews done for the project.

Not long after their marriage, a Mexican consulate was re-established in St. Paul and Ramedo was appointed to the position.

RAMEDO: The fourth consul, Pierce Butler, had passed away. His son, Pierce Butler the third, called me one day and asked if I wouldn't meet him at his office to discuss the need for continued consulate service in this area. At that time there were several Mexican citizens as well as non-Mexican citizens or people of Mexican descent who were going to Pierce Butler for information. . . . The consulate originally was instituted for two reasons. One, for commercial purposes, to stimulate business for Mexico, and two, to serve the Mexican citizens in this area.

CATALINA: I was in charge of the office, receiving the people that came, giving them information that was needed, writing letters, of course, to Mexico, issuing tourist cards to people who were going to visit Mexico, as well as taking care of invoices for the business places, like Minnesota Mining.

Mexican Consul Ramedo Saucedo along with parade chairman Salvador López presented a flag and trophy to Lt. John Picha of the Sheriff Color Guard Unit following the Independence Day parade, September 1971.

Both Ramedo and Catalina said that they used their bilingual skills extensively in the consular duties.

RAMEDO: I must say that this certainly stimulated an interest or aroused a tremendous interest in Mexico for us, since questions were coming in constantly on anything and everything that had to do with Mexico. Therefore we made it a point to travel intensively through Mexico and get to know its history, its people, our ancestors actually, as much as possible.

CATALINA: We had the office at home for the first ten, eleven years, and then the last seven we had it at the Gorman School building, which is on the West Side.

RAMEDO: The Mexican consulate in Chicago, since it is a career consulate and a permanent consulate, is directly involved with the overseeing of a number of offices in the northwestern part as well as the northeastern parts of the United States, for example, Ohio and Indiana and Illinois, of course, and Minnesota, since there are no consulates in North and South Dakota and Iowa. It actually covered this entire area, northern part of the United States. And as a result, from time to time we could go to Chicago to turn in reports and also receive calls from them as well as make calls to them. On a number of occasions we went to Mexico, not only to the American consulate, but also to the Secretary of State's office.

Ramedo and Catalina talked about their families and education.

CATALINA: I have one brother in Minnesota. He is in Crookston, the closest one to me. I have one brother in Texas yet, one brother in California, and two sisters also in Los Angeles. . . . My mother died when I was sixteen and my father in 1972.

RAMEDO: Most of my family is here in Minnesota. As far as cousins and uncles, grandparents, I don't know where they live. My dad became an orphan at the age of ten and left Mexico, arrived here in 1916, and to this date he doesn't know where his six brothers live or whether they still are alive.

CATALINA: Before I was married I went to Rasmussen's Business College and worked after that. Once Ramedo resigned from the consulate, which left me unemployed, so to speak, I decided to go back to business college, and I took an administration training. I have my certificate in business administration in accounting, and I went to work for Northwestern National Bank.

Ramedo talked about how he became a teacher.

RAMEDO: As soon as I graduated from college, receiving my bachelor of arts, I enrolled in law school, and I had been there for a year, and I had just recently gotten married, and we were looking for additional funds since Cathy [Catalina] was working and in a way supporting me to a tremendous degree financially. And then I somehow happened to walk over to look into the College of Education, and someone suggested I speak to a fellow by the name of John Sánchez.

I remember the day I walked into that office at Peik Hall [at the University of Minnesota]. And John Sánchez asked a question after I told him what school I was in. He asked me, "Is your dad a lawyer?" I said, "No." "Well, then, I hope you don't expect people to be breaking down your door and just barging in or waiting in line to come into your office after you hang up your shingle."

And that led me to think a little bit about an immediate employment situation. And that's when the situation opened at University High School, and John invited me to teach there. I was there for six years until 1966.

Ramedo then began teaching at Southwest High School in Minneapolis and discussed the cultural program he took part in.

RAMEDO: Two years ago some of the Chicano students at Franklin Junior High School went to the principal indicating that they weren't receiving enough information on the Mexican American contribution in this country. They weren't getting any Spanish at all. They weren't receiving any cultural information on the Hispanic world at Franklin. At the time, the principal contacted the Chicano Studies Department of the University of Minnesota, which in turn sent a man by the name of Armando Estrella to Franklin once a week. This was in the afternoon between two and three. At the end of one quarter at the university, because Armando's schedule was rather packed, he wasn't able to continue. To continue the encouragement and to avoid there being a gap, the principal then contacted Mr. Jerry Arndt in Minneapolis who in turn asked me if I would be willing to work with those students one day per week. I was then released from my duties at Southwest on Fridays and was able to work with those students as well as students from Sanford and Folwell. So we would meet on Fridays, and basically we labeled it as a Hispanic cultural enrichment program for the Minneapolis Public Schools. The parents were very happy with it. We received several letters of encouragement for continuation of the program. With Armando's help we were able to submit a small proposal to the Minneapolis Public Schools and this year [1977] we were able to work a little stronger with the program. So currently then, it's the Hispanic Cultural Enrichment Program designed for children of Hispanic background but not strictly limited to them.

Through work at the consulate and with the school programs, Ramedo and Catalina did some traveling in Mexico and encouraged others, particularly students, to do likewise.

RAMEDO: Being involved with Spanish, actually my full-time position, we became so interested in my travels through Mexico that I couldn't help but let the students know and help develop a better understanding of another person's culture. It's all part of the language, as far as I'm concerned. And the books, of course, give you a certain limited amount of information, and my whole-hearted enthusiasm was to encourage the students to participate in some type of a travel program. We would go summers and also lately, during the past four or five school years, during the school year.

We went to Mexico City. Also Guadalajara, the second largest city, and a small town by the name of Patzcuaro. I selected these three towns or cities, one, to give them [the students] a picture of how people live in a city of ten million—Mexico City, secondly, a more peaceful, more Spanish colonial-type architecturally designed city like Guadalajara, and thirdly, a fishing village, a little more remote, out of the way, difficult to get to such as Patzcuaro with cobblestone streets and roosters crowing in the morning and the typical atmosphere say that existed maybe three or four hundred years ago.

Source: Interview of Ramedo and Catalina Saucedo by Juan Sánchez, April 6, 1977, OH, MHS.

For Further Reading

Holmquist, June D., ed. *They Chose Minnesota: A Survey of the State's Ethnic Groups.* St. Paul: Minnesota Historical Society Press, 1981.

Kaplan, Anne R., Marjorie A. Hoover, and Willard B. Moore. *The Minnesota Ethnic Food Book.* St. Paul: Minnesota Historical Society Press, 1986. "The Mexicans," 48–66, 282–95.

López-Santamaría, Maya. *Música de la Raza: Mexican and Chicano Music in Minnesota.* St. Paul: Minnesota Historical Society Press, 1999.

Saucedo, Ramedo J., comp. *Mexican Americans in Minnesota: An Introduction to Historical Sources.* St. Paul: Minnesota Historical Society, 1977.

Valdés, Dionicio N. *Al Norte: Agricultural Workers in the Great Lakes Region, 1917–1970.* Austin: University of Texas Press, 1991.

———. *Barrios Norteños: St. Paul and Midwestern Mexican Communities in the Twentieth Century.* Austin: University of Texas Press, 2000.

Notes

1. *Minneapolis Star Tribune*, May 6, 2003.

2. Alice Lilliequist Sickels, "The Mexican Nationality Community of St. Paul, May 1936," 8, International Institute Papers, Box 30, folder 200, Immigration History Research Center, University of Minnesota, Minneapolis (hereafter II, IHRC).

3. George T. Edson, "Mexicans in Our Northcentral States," 1927, copy in Bancroft Library, University of California—Berkeley; Neighborhood House, Annual Report, June 1939, Box 1, folder: History and Purpose, General, Neighborhood House Papers, Minnesota Historical Society (hereafter NH, MHS).

4. George T. Edson, "Mexicans in Minneapolis and St. Paul," 1927, copy in Paul Schuster Taylor Papers, 1660–1997, Bancroft Library, University of California—Berkeley; *Minneapolis Star Tribune*, Apr. 30, 1999.

5. Edson, "Minneapolis and St. Paul"; Neighborhood House, St. Paul, Minnesota, 1938, folder 380, Social Welfare History Archives, University of Minnesota, Minneapolis.

6. Edson, "Minneapolis and St. Paul."

7. Neighborhood House, Board of Directors Minutes, Apr. 14, 1932, and Feb. 10, 1936, Box 1, NH, MHS; Sickels, "Mexican Nationality Community," 8; Sickels, "Mexican Nationality Community," 6.

8. II, IHRC, Box 25, folder 451.

9. Sickels, "Mexican Nationality Community" 19.

10. Abraham Hoffman, *Unwanted Mexican Americans in the Great Depression: Repatriation Pressures, 1929–1939* (Tucson: University of Arizona Press, 1974), 126.

11. Neighborhood House, Notes from Secretary's Minutes, Nov. 10, 1932, folder: History and Purpose, General, and Board of Directors Minutes, Nov. 10, 1932, Box 1, NH, MHS; Minnesota Governor, Governor's Interracial Commission, *The Mexican in Minnesota* (St. Paul, 1948), 41; *St. Paul Daily News*, June 15, 1937.

12. Sickels, "Mexican Nationality Community," 12.

13. Neighborhood House, Board Minutes, Feb. 14, 1924, Box 1, folder: Board Minutes, 1918–1928, and Annual Report, June 1939, Box 1, folder: History and Purpose, General, NH, MHS.

14. Sickels, "Mexican Nationality Community," 15.

15. International Institute and Neighborhood House, "A Study of the Mexican Community in St. Paul, September, 1946," 7, Box 13, folder 201, and Box 27, folder 1580, II, IHRC; Sickels, "Mexican Nationality Community," 17.

16. International Institute and Neighborhood House, "Mexican Survey," St. Paul, 1935, p. 3, 5, Box 13, folder: 200, IHRC.

17. International Institute, "Mexican Survey," 3; IHRC, II, Box 31, folder 713.

18. Dionicio Valdés, *Al Norte: Agricultural Workers in the Great Lakes Region, 1917–1970* (Austin: University of Texas Press, 1991), 38–47.

19. Stanley White to J. R. Steelman, folder 196/139, U.S. Mediation and Conciliation Service, Record Group 280, National Archives, Washington, D.C.;

Minnesota Governor, *Mexican in Minnesota*, 23; Neighborhood House, Board of Directors Minutes, May 13, 1937, Box 1, Minutes 1933–1939, NH, MHS; Louise Lambert, "Tank Town: Mexicans in Minnesota," *Hamline Piper*, May 1935, p. 24–31; Neighborhood House, "Survey of Homes and Businesses, Sixth Ward, 1936," Box 13, folder: Studies, NH, MHS; Dionicio Valdés, *Barrios Norteños: St. Paul and Midwestern Mexican Communities in the Twentieth Century* (Autin: University of Texas Press, 2000), 112.

20. Interview Sr. Juan Gómez by author, Mar. 18, 1995, notes in author's possession.

21. IHRC, II, Box 25, folder 1281, and Box 30, folder 744.

22. "Women in Steel," *Life*, Aug. 9, 1945, p. 75–81; Richard Santillán, "Rosita the Riveter: Midwest Mexican American Women during World War II, 1941–1945," *Perspectives in Mexican American Studies* 2 (1989): 115–47.

23. Minnesota Migrant Reports Summary of 1944 Activities, Box 41, folder: Midwest 1940s, Home Missions Council Papers, Presbyterian Historical Society, Philadelphia (hereafter HMC, PHS); George W. Hill to Clarence Hurt, June 9, 1943, folder: Farm labor 53—certification (Minnesota), War Food Administration, Record Group 224, NA; *Duluth Herald*, June, 1944 (article and picture of Mexicans working on the Northern Pacific Railroad).

24. "Local employment agent," Apr. 30, 1947, folder: migrants, Mexican American Community in St. Paul Papers (hereafter MAC), MHS.

25. Migrant Work in Minnesota, 1946, Box 41, folder: Midwest 1940s, HMC, PHS.

26. Treatment of Workers in Rosemont Cannery, Faribault, Minnesota (1947), folder: Laborers 1, RG 224, NA; Report of Dorothy Knowles, Minnesota: July, August 1945, Box 41, folder: Midwest 1940s, HMC, PHS; Minnesota Governor, *Mexican in Minnesota*, 7.

27. International Institute, "Study of the Mexican Community," 8–9.

28. David E. and Lila Henley, *Minnesota and Her Migratory Workers* (Minneapolis: Migrant Committee of the Minnesota Council of Churches, 1950), 25.

29. IHRC, II, Box 30, folder 744; International Institute, "Study of the Mexican Community," 10–11.

30. Valdés, *Barrios*, 179–82.

31. Interview Sr. Alfredo González, May 16, 1995; "The Report of the University of Minnesota Task Force on Chicano Concerns," Box 2, folder: University of Minnesota 1977–1978, Irene Gómez Bethke Papers, MHS.

32. Committee on Institutional Cooperation, Full Time, Tenured and Tenure-Track Faculty at CIC Universities by Race and Ethnicity 1993, 1995, 1997, and 1999 Final Reports; Chicano Studies Department, University of Minnesota, "Department Plan 2002," Nov. 19, 2001.

33. *St. Cloud Times*, May 8, 1995; *La Prensa de Minnesota*, May 18, 1995.

34. *Minneapolis Star Tribune*, Apr. 30, 1999, Nov. 1, 1998.

35. "What is MIA—Past and Present," Box 2, folder: Migrants in Action, Historical Sketch, Bethke Papers; Minnesota Migrant Council, 1975–1976 Biennial Report, Box 1, folder: Research/Issues: Vietnam, MAC Papers; *Fargo-Moorhead Forum*, Apr. 5, 1992; Interviews of Peter Moreno, Aug. 6, 1976, and José Valdez, June 21, 1976, transcripts, Mexican American History Project, MHS.

36. *St. Paul Pioneer Press*, July 2, 1969,

July 3, 1969; *Minneapolis Tribune,* Aug. 8, 1971.

37. *Minneapolis Star,* Nov. 22, 1978; *Minneapolis Tribune,* Aug. 8, 1971.

38. José Trejo, *Children of Misfortune* (Austin, Minn., 1962); June Cedarleaf to A. E. Ramberg, June 9, 1955, Industrial Commission of Minnesota, folder: Migrants (1954–1975), MHS.

39. *Minneapolis Tribune,* Aug. 8, 1971.

40. *Minneapolis Star,* Nov. 22, 1978, Nov. 20, 1978.

41. *St. Paul Pioneer Press,* July 3, June 29, June 30, 1969; Ann Baker, "Machines to end need for migrants," undated clipping, folder: Migrants (2), MAC; *Minneapolis Tribune,* Aug. 8, 1971, June 22, 1969.

42. *Fargo-Moorhead Forum,* July 26, 1992; *St. Cloud Daily Times,* Feb. 12, 1975; *St. Paul Pioneer Press,* Oct. 11, 1974; *Minneapolis Star,* Sept. 13, 1974.

43. *Fargo-Moorhead Forum,* June 1, 1989; *Fargo Forum,* Dec. 17, 1990.

44. *Minneapolis Star,* Nov. 22, 1978.

45. *Grand Forks Herald,* May 27, 1990; *St. Paul Pioneer Press,* June 7, 1992; Minnesota Department of Human Services, "Use of public assistance by migrant farm workers in the Red River Valley," February 1990, folder: politics, Spanish Speaking Affairs Council, St. Paul (hereafter SSAC); *Minneapolis Star Tribune,* Sept. 2, 1985.

46. *Minneapolis Star Tribune,* Sept. 2, 1985.

47. *St. Paul Pioneer Press,* July 22, 1992.

48. *Minneapolis Star Tribune,* Apr. 30, 1999; *St. Paul Pioneer Press,* Nov. 30, 2002.

49. *Minneapolis Star Tribune,* June 3, 2000, Nov. 30, 2000, June 3, 2000, Jan. 28, 2000, Oct. 11, 2001.

50. *Mankato Free Press,* Nov. 24, 1990.

51. *Minneapolis Star Tribune,* Oct. 1, 1992, Nov. 26, 1989; *Rochester Post-Bulletin,* June 24, 1992; *St. Cloud Times,* July 2, 1989; *Chicago Tribune,* Dec. 24, 1990.

52. *Rochester Post-Bulletin,* Dec. 1, 1990; Letter to editor, *Fargo-Moorhead Forum,* May 24, 1990; *Minneapolis Star Tribune,* June 9, 1992.

53. *St. Paul Pioneer Press,* Apr. 7, 1991.

54. *Rochester Post-Bulletin,* Dec. 1, 1990; *Mankato Free Press,* July 26, 1993; *Minneapolis Star Tribune,* Nov. 26, 1989.

55. *Rochester Post-Bulletin,* June 24, 1992; *Minneapolis Star Tribune,* Aug. 12, 1990, June 11, 1989; *Minneapolis Star,* Nov. 22, 23, 1978; Sam Hernández, "General Background of the Mexican American," (1973), Box 17, folder: Hispanics, NH, MHS.

56. *St. Paul Dispatch,* May 7, 1976; *Fargo-Moorhead Forum,* July 26, 1992; *St. Paul Pioneer Press,* Mar. 27, 2003.

57. *Minneapolis Star Tribune,* June 19, 1991; *St. Paul Pioneer Press,* Nov. 25, 1993; www.usagnet.com (accessed Nov. 29, 2004).

58. *Los Angeles Times,* Apr. 7, 1991; *Minneapolis Star Tribune,* Oct. 1, 1992.

59. *Fargo Forum,* Aug. 4, 1991.

60. *Minneapolis Star Tribune,* Apr. 16, 1993, May 5, 1993; *St. Paul Pioneer Press,* Apr. 27, 2003.

61. *Minneapolis Star Tribune,* Oct. 1, 1992, Dec. 12, 1990; *Mankato Free Press,* Nov. 24, 1990.

62. *Minneapolis Star Tribune,* Oct. 1, 1992, Oct. 11, 1992.

63. *Minneapolis Star Tribune,* Apr. 16, 1993, Dec. 12, 1990.

64. *Minneapolis Star Tribune,* Nov. 15, 1999.

65. *Minneapolis Star Tribune,* May 5, 2001, Nov. 15, 1999.

66. *St. Paul Pioneer Press,* Apr. 27, 2003, Sept. 19, 2002; *Minneapolis Star Tribune,*

Sept. 23, 2002; www.districtdelsol.com (accessed Nov. 30, 2004); www.clues.org (accessed Nov. 30, 2004).

67. *Minneapolis Star Tribune,* Apr. 1, 2001; Valdés, *Barrios,* 224.

68. *Minneapolis Star Tribune,* Apr. 30, 1999, June 3, 2000, Nov. 30, 2000, Sept. 7, 2000; *St. Paul Pioneer Press,* Nov. 30, 2001.

69. *Minneapolis Star Tribune,* Mar. 29, 2001, Apr. 1, 2001, Mar. 20, 2003; James Kielkopf, *The Economic Impact of Undocumented Workers in Minnesota* (Minneapolis: HACER, 2000).

70. *Minneapolis Star Tribune,* Jan. 11, 2003; *St. Paul Pioneer Press,* Dec. 19, 2002, Sept. 28, 2000, Apr. 28, 2003.

71. *St. Paul Pioneer Press,* Apr. 2, 2001; *Minneapolis Star Tribune,* Sept. 16, 1999, Feb. 22, 2001, Sept. 7, 2000.

72. *Grand Forks Herald,* Apr. 2, 1989; *Minneapolis Tribune,* Aug. 8, 1971; *Redwood Gazette,* Aug. 19, 1975.

73. Sallie Kyle, "Education Unit Created to Aid Migrant Children," *Update,* Sept. 1975, p. 6; *Minneapolis Tribune,* Aug. 8, 1971, June 22, 1969.

74. *St. Paul Pioneer Press,* June 29, 1969; *Minneapolis Star Tribune,* May 2, 1990.

75. *St. Paul Pioneer Press,* May 3, 1990, June 7, 1992; *Detroit Lakes–Becker County Record,* Dec. 17, 1989; *Fargo-Moorhead Forum,* May 20, 1992, July 26, 1992.

76. *Minneapolis Star Tribune,* Dec. 13, 1987, Apr. 4, 1993; *Chicago Tribune,* Dec. 24, 1990; *St. Paul Pioneer Press,* Dec. 30, 1987; *Redwood Gazette,* Aug. 19, 1975; "Hispanic Population Grows," National Public Radio Weekend Edition broadcast, Mar. 1, 1992; *Grand Forks Herald,* June 8, 1992.

77. *St. Paul Pioneer Press,* May 28, 1989; *St. Cloud Times,* July 2, 1989; *Minneapolis Tribune,* Aug. 8, 1971; *Rochester Post-Bulletin,* May 9, 1991.

78. *Minneapolis Star Tribune,* Sept. 6, 1988, Dec. 13, 1987.

79. Spanish Speaking Affairs Council, *SSAC 1992 Biennium Report,* SSAC files; *West Central Tribune (Willmar),* Aug. 17, 1991.

80. *Minneapolis Star Tribune,* Sept. 5, 1993, May 2, 1990; Minnesota Department of Human Services, "Use of Public Assistance by Migrant Workers in the Red River Valley," February 1990, Politics folder, SSAC.

81. *St. Paul Pioneer Press,* Dec. 30, 1987; *Fargo-Moorhead Forum,* June 24, 1992; *Minneapolis Star Tribune,* Feb. 4, 1993.

82. *St. Paul Pioneer Press,* Oct. 1, 1993; *Chicago Tribune,* Dec. 24, 1990; *Minneapolis Star Tribune,* Dec. 21, 1993.

83. *Minneapolis Star Tribune,* July 2, 1990.

84. *Minneapolis Star Tribune,* Oct. 1, 1992, Oct. 11, 1992, Oct. 21, 1992.

85. *St. Paul Pioneer Press,* Nov. 1, 2000, Oct. 2, 2002.

86. *Fargo-Moorhead Forum,* May 21, 1989; *Minneapolis Star Tribune,* Apr. 4, 1993, Sept. 3, 1993, May 28, 1989, Apr. 4, 1993, Apr., 4, 1993; *Mankato Free Press,* Nov. 24, 1990.

87. *Minneapolis Star Tribune,* Feb. 12, 2001, May 29, 2001, May 10, 2002, July 17, 2000; *St. Paul Pioneer Press,* May 18, 2003, June 30, 2003; www.pnn.org/ed/sanmiguel (accessed Dec. 7, 2004).

88. *Minneapolis Star Tribune,* Jan. 25, 1990; *St. Paul Pioneer Press,* Jan. 10, 2001.

89. *Grand Forks Herald,* June 8, 1992; *Minneapolis Star Tribune,* Apr. 27, 1993.

90. *Minneapolis Star Tribune,* July 16, 1988, Aug. 9, 1992.

91. *Minneapolis Star Tribune,* Apr. 16, 1993, May 5, 1993, Aug. 18, 1993, Aug. 21, 1993, Nov. 20, 1992, Sept. 21, 1993, Oct. 13,

1993; *St. Paul Pioneer Press,* Apr. 24, 1993, Aug. 18, 1993; *Marshall Independent,* May 5, 1993.

92. *Minneapolis Star Tribune,* Nov. 20, 1992; *Marshall Independent,* May 8, 1993.

93. *Minneapolis Star Tribune,* Apr. 12, 1991; Bill McDonald to Raul de Ande (sp.), April 19, 1990, enclosed with minutes of SSAC Meeting, St. Paul, July 28, 1990, SSAC; *Rochester Post-Bulletin,* Feb. 16, 1988.

94. *Mankato Free Press,* Jan. 3, 1991.

95. Interview of Bill Villareal, July 26, 1976, OH, MHS; *Minneapolis Star Tribune,* Apr. 27, 1993; Chris Williams, "Hombres of Summer," *Associated Press,* Sept. 7, 2002.

96. *West Central Tribune,* May 12, 1993; *St. Paul Pioneer Press,* Feb. 18, 1991.

97. *Marshall Independent,* May 5, 1993, May 8, 1993; *Minneapolis Star Tribune,* May 8, 1993.

98. *Minneapolis Star Tribune,* Aug. 7, 2000; www.archspm.org (accessed Dec. 7, 2004); www.dnu.org (accessed Nov. 29, 2004); www.dow.org (accessed Nov. 29, 2004).

99. *St. Paul Pioneer Press,* Mar. 26, 2000.

100. *St. Paul Pioneer Press,* June 13, 2004, Dec. 1, 2004; *Minneapolis Star Tribune,* Dec. 1, 2004.

Notes to Sidebars

Separating a Mother and Daughter, p. 12: IHRC, II, Box 34, folder 418.

Packinghouse Workers, p. 27: International Institute, "Study of the Mexican Community," 9; IHRC, Box 27, folder 1037.

Mexican Music, p. 60: Maya López-Santamaría, *Música de la Raza: Mexican and Chicano Music in Minnesota* (St. Paul: Minnesota Historical Society Press, 1999).

Family Foodways, p. 68: Anne R. Kaplan, Marjorie A. Hoover, and Willard B. Moore, *The Minnesota Ethnic Food Book* (St. Paul: Minnesota Historical Society Press, 1986), 48–66.

A Mexican Police Officer, p. 71: *West Central Tribune,* July 23, 1992; *Minneapolis Star Tribune,* Oct. 11, 2001, Aug. 9, 1992, Jan. 3, 1993, Oct. 9, 11, 1992, Aug. 9, 1992.

Soccer, p. 75: Interview of Lalo Sánchez by Ramedo Saucedo, July 23, 1975, OH, MHS.

Organizing a Union Local, p. 76: St. Paul Pioneer Press, Mar. 26, 2000, Oct. 16, 1999; Interview of Rosario, by author, 2000, notes in author's possession; Dionicio Valdés, "The Holiday In(n)cident: Mexican Immigration, Service Sector Employment and Union Struggle in Minneapolis," in *Illusion of Borders: The National Presence of Mexicanos in the United States,* ed. Gilberto García and Jerry García (Dubuque, Iowa: Kendall/Hunt Pub. Co., 2002), 27–40; *Washington Post,* Dec. 6, 1999; *Minneapolis Star Tribune,* Oct. 19, Oct. 20, 1999, Jan. 7, 10, 28, 2000.

Index

Page numbers in italic refer to pictures and captions.

Picture Credits

Names of the photographers, when known, are in parentheses.

Front cover, back cover, page x, 3 (Russell Lee, Farm Security Administration), 6, 7 (*St. Paul Dispatch*), 8, 10, 13, 14 (Kenneth García Family Photos), 17, 19, 21, 24, 25, 26, 28 (Kenneth García Family Photos), 29, 30 (Kenneth García Family Photos), 33, 36 (Governor's Human Rights Commission), 37 (Governor's Human Rights Commission), 38 (Jerome Liebling), 42 (both Steven A. Schluter), 45 (Governor's Human Rights Commission), 49 (all Jerome Liebling), 55 (Morton), 56 (both), 57 (Jack Gillis), 60 (Edward G. Edmundson), 68 (*St. Paul Dispatch-Pioneer Press*), 74, 75, 82—Minnesota Historical Society

Page 20—courtesy of the Avaloz family

Acknowledgments

This essay revises the late Susan M. Diebold's chapter, "The Mexicans," in *They Chose Minnesota*. Her work remains a valuable resource for Mexicans in Minnesota. The author would like to thank Chris Taylor, Rebecca Rubinstein, and Mariesa Bus for picture research; the Avaloz family for loaning a family photograph; and Jerome Liebling for giving permission for his photographs to be used. Deborah Miller encouraged this project in its early stages and provided valuable comments on the manuscript. Sally Rubinstein saw the project through the editorial process.

Minnesotans can trace their families and their state's heritage to a multitude of ethnic groups. *The People of Minnesota* series tells each group's story in a compact, handsomely illustrated, and accessible paperback. Readers will learn about the group's accomplishments, ethnic organizations, settlement patterns, and occupations. Each book includes a personal story of one person or family, told through a diary, a letter, or an oral history.

In his introduction to the series, Bill Holm reminds us why these stories are as important as ever: "To be ethnic, somehow, is to be human. Neither can we escape it, nor should we want to. You cannot interest yourself in the lives of your neighbors if you don't take sufficient interest in your own."

This series is based on the critically acclaimed book *They Chose Minnesota: A Survey of the State's Ethnic Groups* (Minnesota Historical Society Press). The volumes in *The People of Minnesota* bring each group's story up to date and add dozens of photographs to inform and enhance the telling.

Books in the series include *Irish in Minnesota, Jews in Minnesota, Norwegians in Minnesota, African Americans in Minnesota, Germans in Minnesota, Chinese in Minnesota,* and *Swedes in Minnesota.*

Bill Holm is the grandson of four Icelandic immigrants to Minneota, Minnesota, where he still lives. He is the author of eight books including *Eccentric Island: Travels Real and Imaginary* and *Coming Home Crazy.* When he is not practicing the piano or on the road circuit-riding for literature, he teaches at Southwest State University in Marshall, Minnesota.

About the Author

Dionicio Valdés is a history professor and senior researcher at the Julian Samora Research Institute at Michigan State University. He is the author of *Barrios Norteños: St. Paul and Midwestern Mexican Communities in the Twentieth Century* and *Al Norte: Agricultural Workers in the Great Lakes Region, 1917–1970.*